D1090347

NEW ORLEANS SAINTS

BY ALEX MONNIG

Published by The Child's World®
1980 Lookout Drive • Mankato, MN 56003-1705
800-599-READ • www.childsworld.com

Acknowledgments
The Child's World®: Mary Berendes, Publishing Director
Red Line Editorial: Editorial direction
The Design Lab: Design
Amnet: Production

Design Element: Dean Bertoncelj/Shutterstock Images
Photographs ©: Tim Sharp/AP Images, cover; Rick
Osentoski/AP Images, 5; Mike Groll/AP Images, 7; NFL
Photos/AP Images, 9, 29; Bill Haber/AP Images, 11, 19, 27;
Shutterstock Images, 13; Jonathan Bachman/AP Images,
14-15; David J. Phillip/AP Images, 17; Gerald Herbert/AP
Images, 21; Paul Jasienski/AP Images, 23; Michael Perez/
AP Images, 25

ISBN 9781634070133
LCCN 2014959718

Printed in the United States of America
Mankato, MN
Month, 2015
PAO2265

ABOUT THE AUTHOR

Alex Monnig is a freelance journalist from St. Louis, Missouri, who now lives in Sydney, Australia. He has traveled across the world to cover sporting events in China, India, Singapore, New Zealand, and Scotland. No matter where he is, he always makes time to keep up to date with his favorite teams from his hometown.

TABLE OF CONTENTS

GO, SAINTS!

T hings have not always been smooth for the New Orleans Saints. They did not make the **playoffs** their first 20 years. They were often one of the worst teams in the league. But the team has a special bond with its fans. The Saints helped the city after it was hit by Hurricane Katrina in 2005. A few years later the Saints were champions. Let's meet the Saints.

Saints quarterback Drew Brees (9) prepares to start a play against the Detroit Lions on October 19, 2014.

WHO ARE THE SAINTS?

The New Orleans Saints play in the National Football **League** (NFL). They are one of the 32 teams in the NFL. The NFL includes the American Football Conference (AFC) and the National Football Conference. The winner of the NFC plays the winner of the AFC in the **Super Bowl**. The Saints play in the South Division of the NFC. New Orleans has been to the Super Bowl once. The 2009 Saints won the big game.

Saints cornerback Tracy Porter returns an interception for a touchdown against the Indianapolis Colts in Super Bowl XLIV on February 7, 2010.

WHERE THEY CAME FROM

David F. Dixon wanted an NFL team in New Orleans. He hosted **exhibition** NFL games to show that people there loved football. The NFL gave New Orleans an **expansion** team. The Saints entered the league in 1967. Fans chose the team's nickname. It was a good choice. The franchise was awarded to New Orleans on All Saints Day. The city has a large Catholic population. The Saints did not make the playoffs until 1987. Coach Sean Payton and quarterback Drew Brees arrived in New Orleans in 2006. It started the team's most successful stretch. Payton built a great offense. The Saints became one of the best teams in the league.

Saints wide receiver Eric Martin catches a touchdown pass against the Minnesota Vikings during a playoff game on January 3, 1988.

WHO THEY PLAY

The Saints play 16 games each season. With so few games, each one is important. Every year, the Saints play two games against each of the other three teams in their division. They are the Atlanta Falcons, Carolina Panthers, and Tampa Bay Buccaneers. The Falcons and Saints are **rivals**. They have had some high-scoring battles.

Saints wide receiver Jalen Saunders runs with the ball against the NFC South Division rival Carolina Panthers on December 7, 2014.

WHERE THEY PLAY

The Saints played at Tulane University until 1974. They moved into the Louisiana Superdome in 1975. It is now called the Mercedes-Benz Superdome. The **stadium** served a bigger purpose in 2005. Parts of New Orleans flooded when Hurricane Katrina hit that year. Thousands of homes were destroyed. So people went to the Superdome for shelter. That season the Saints played their home games elsewhere. New Orleans has hosted the Super Bowl 10 times. Three of those were at Tulane Stadium. Seven were at the Superdome.

The Mercedes-Benz Superdome seats 72,003 fans. That makes it one of the biggest stadiums in the NFL.

THE FOOTBALL FIELD

BENCH AREA

20-YARD LINE

GOAL LINE

END ZONE

END LINE

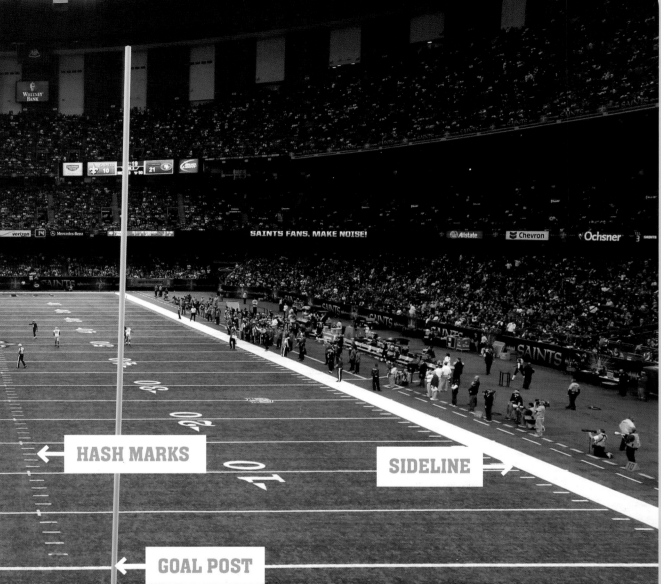

HASH MARKS

SIDELINE

GOAL POST

BIG DAYS

2000—The Saints won a playoff game for the first time. They beat the St. Louis Rams on December 30. St. Louis did not make it easy. The Rams scored three **touchdowns** in the final 10 minutes. But the Saints held on to win 31-28.

2006—New Orleans met the rival Atlanta Falcons on September 25 on *Monday Night Football*. It was their first game at the Superdome after Hurricane Katrina. The stadium was rocking. The Saints blocked the Falcons' first punt and recovered it for a touchdown. New Orleans won 23-3.

2010—The 2009 Saints won the team's first Super Bowl on February 7. They beat the Indianapolis

Quarterback Drew Brees celebrates with the Vince Lombardi Trophy after leading the Saints to victory in Super Bowl XLIV on February 7, 2010.

Colts 31–17. Defensive back Tracy Porter made a key late play. He intercepted a pass from Colts quarterback Peyton Manning with 3:24 to go. Porter returned the interception for a touchdown to seal the win.

TOUGH DAYS

1980—Coach Dick Nolan was fired after the Saints started the season 0-12. The team finished 1-15. New Orleans did not win until its 15th game.

2005—The Superdome was full of people who needed help after Hurricane Katrina. New Orleans could not play home games there. The Saints played one home game in New York, three in Texas, and four at Louisiana State University.

2012—It was a dark time for the Saints. In 2009 some New Orleans players had tried to hurt opponents on purpose. They were paid extra money—or "bounties"—

A Saints fan wears a bag over his head in embarrassment during the team's miserable 1980 season.

to do so. The NFL punished the Saints for that. Some players were suspended and coach Sean Payton was banned for a year.

MEET THE FANS

Fans lined up to buy Saints tickets before the team had even played a game. They still love the Saints today. New Orleans is famous for jazz music. One well-known song is "When the Saints Go Marching In." The song is often played at Saints games. "Who dat?" is a popular saying among fans. It is short for "Who dat say dey gonna beat dem Saints?"

Saints fans are known for dressing up and always having a good time at games.

HEROES THEN

Linebacker Rickey Jackson was the first player to spend most of his career with the Saints and make the Pro Football Hall of Fame. He was third on the career **sacks** list when he retired in 1995. Tackle Willie Roaf was a great quarterback protector. He spent 1993-2001 with New Orleans. Roaf made seven **Pro Bowls** in a row during that time. He is also in the Hall of Fame. Archie Manning was a star quarterback from 1971-1982. He is also the father of Denver Broncos quarterback Peyton Manning and New York Giants quarterback Eli Manning.

Offensive tackle Willie Roaf gets in position to make a block for the Saints during a game against the Phoenix Cardinals on October 31, 1993.

HEROES NOW

Quarterback Drew Brees and coach Sean Payton lead the high-scoring Saints offense. Brees is not very tall for a quarterback. But he is still one of the best. He made the Pro Bowl seven times from 2006 to 2013. Brees led the NFL in passing touchdowns and passing yards four times each in that span. Running back Mark Ingram developed into a star. The Saints picked him in the first round of the 2011 NFL Draft. Ingram made his first Pro Bowl in 2014.

Saints running back Mark Ingram runs with the ball in a playoff game against the Philadelphia Eagles on January 4, 2014.

GEARING UP

NFL players wear team uniforms. They wear helmets and pads to keep them safe. Cleats help them make quick moves and run fast. Some players wear extra gear for protection.

THE FOOTBALL

NFL footballs are made of leather. Under the leather is a lining that fills with air to give the ball its shape. The leather has bumps or "pebbles." These help players grip the ball. Laces help players control their throws. Footballs are also called "pigskins" because some of the first balls were made from pig bladders. Today they are made of leather from cows.

Saints wide receiver Marques Colston runs with the ball against the Arizona Cardinals on September 22, 2013.

HELMET

SHOULDER PADS

GLOVES

THIGH PADS

FOOTBALL

CLEATS

SPORTS STATS

ere are some of the all-time career records for the New Orleans Saints. All the stats are through the 2014 season:

RUSHING YARDS

Deuce McAllister 6,096

George Rogers 4,267

RECEPTIONS

Marques Colston 666

Eric Martin 532

TOTAL TOUCHDOWNS

Marques Colston 68

Deuce McAllister 55

INTERCEPTIONS

Dave Waymer 37

Tom Myers 36

SACKS

Rickey Jackson 115

Wayne Martin 82.5

POINTS

Morten Andersen 1,318

John Carney 768

Saints quarterback Archie Manning drops back to pass against the Los Angeles Rams on November 11, 1973.

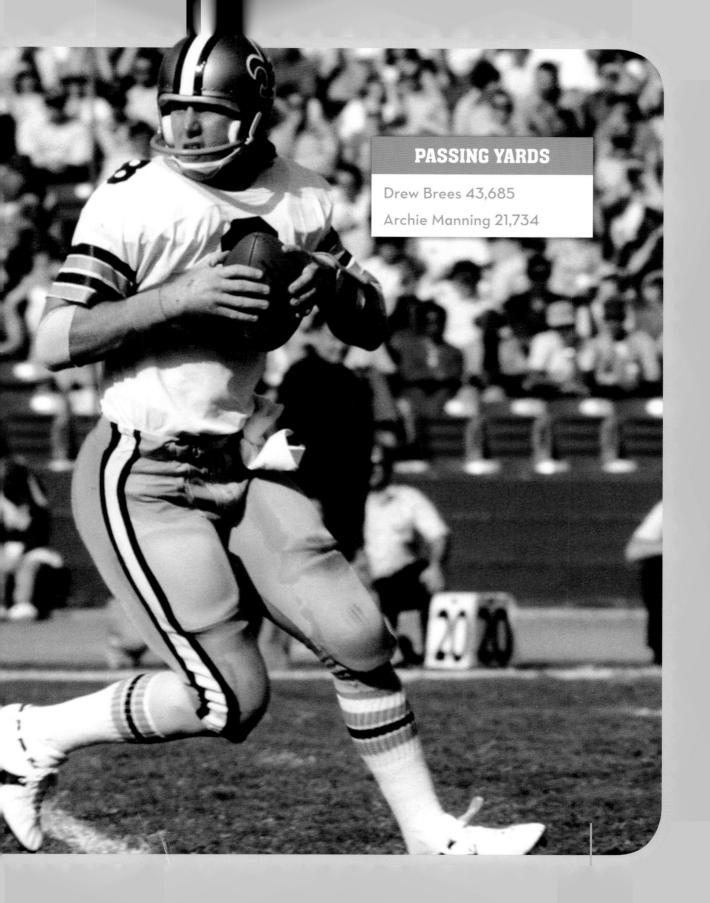

PASSING YARDS

Drew Brees 43,685

Archie Manning 21,734

GLOSSARY

exhibition a game that doesn't count toward teams' rankings or records

expansion when a league grows by adding a team or teams

league an organization of sports teams that compete against each other

playoffs a series of games after the regular season that decides which two teams play in the Super Bowl

Pro Bowl the NFL's All-Star game, in which the best players in the league compete

rivals teams whose games bring out the greatest emotion between the players and the fans on both sides

sacks when the quarterback is tackled behind the line of scrimmage before he can throw the ball

stadium a building with a field and seats for fans where teams play

Super Bowl the championship game of the NFL, played between the winner of the AFC and the NFC

touchdown a play in which the ball is held in the other team's end zone, resulting in six points

FIND OUT MORE

IN THE LIBRARY

Frisch, Aaron. *Super Bowl Champions: New Orleans Saints*. Mankato, MN: Creative Education, 2014.

Sandler, Michael. *Drew Brees and the New Orleans Saints: Super Bowl XLIV*. New York, NY: Bearport Publishing, 2010.

Whiting, Jim. *The Story of the New Orleans Saints*. Mankato, MN: Creative Education, 2014.

ON THE WEB

Visit our Web site for links about the New Orleans Saints:
childsworld.com/links

Note to Parents, Teachers, and Librarians: We routinely verify our Web links to make sure they are safe and active sites. So encourage your readers to check them out!

INDEX

Parks: Design and Management

Parks: Design and Management

Leonard E. Phillips

McGraw-Hill

New York   San Francisco   Washington, D.C.   Auckland   Bogotá
Caracas   Lisbon   London   Madrid   Mexico City   Milan
Montreal   New Delhi   San Juan   Singapore
Sydney   Tokyo   Toronto

Library of Congress Cataloging-in-Publication Data

Phillips, Leonard E.
   Parks : design and management / Leonard E. Phillips.
      p.   cm.
   Includes index.
   ISBN 0-07-049871-7 (hardcover : acid-free paper)
   1. Parks—Management.   2. Parks—Design and construction.
3. Playgrounds—Design and construction.   I. Title.
SB486.M35P48   1995
363.6'8—dc20   95-37116
                                     CIP

McGraw-Hill

A Division of The McGraw-Hill Companies

1 2 3 4 5 6 7 8 9 0 DOC/DOC 9 0 0 9 8 7 6 5

ISBN 0-07-049871-7

The sponsoring editor for this book was Hal Crawford, the editing supervisor was Bernard Onken, and the production supervisor was Suzanne Rapcavage. It was set in Palatino by North Market Street Graphics.

Printed and bound by R.R. Donnelley & Sons Company.

McGraw-Hill books are available at special quantity discounts to use as premiums and sales promotions, or for use in corporate training programs. For more information, please write to the Director of Special Sales, McGraw-Hill, 11 West 19th Street, New York, NY 10011. Or contact your local bookstore.

This book is printed on acid-free paper.

Contents

Preface

The proper design and management of parks is the recurring theme of every chapter of this book. Successful parks and playgrounds require good design, proper management, and supportive people. This book has been written to provide guidance in proper design as well as tips on improving the management of any public open space.

Several books have been written on the general subject of landscape management but few ever mention shortcuts for increasing efficiency or productivity. This book has therefore been prepared to provide incentive and direction for finding efficient solutions to specific maintenance problems. It will serve as a guide to aid the experienced park or landscape maintenance supervisor. Throughout the book, illustrations provide many examples of successful solutions to common problems.

In this age of tight budgets, every park manager should be seeking shortcuts to increase productivity by accomplishing the same task with fewer resources or more tasks for the same amount of money. Public landscape designers must step back, look at the overall scope of a project and determine the design; the lands to be maintained; the money, materials, and labor available to do the job; the people involved in the project; and the most efficient way to do specific tasks.

Remember, there is almost nothing that cannot be done more efficiently. The assignment of park managers, therefore, is to keep searching for the most efficient approach for every task we do. It is the goal of this book to serve as a guide to achieving that goal.

Leonard E. Phillips

Acknowledgments

The support of my two assistants must be acknowledged. Ron Despres, Wellesley's Town Arborist, and Cricket Vlass, Wellesley's Horticulturalist, have both reviewed various portions of this book for technical accuracy. Ron has also been especially instrumental in developing many of the innovative ideas used to illustrate various parts of this book. A special thank you must also be extended to Irene Kent who spent so many hours typing and revising the book. She had to endure at least three major revisions after the original text was gathered from about twenty different sources. She brought it all together with great success. I must also thank my family for being so patient. My wife Carol and three daughters—Kristine, Suzanne, and Michelle—all had to endure my absence while I wrote and rewrote this book.

To all of you, a special thank you.

PART 1
Design

How to Design a Successful Park

Parks are positive elements of our urban environment and landscape. The properly designed park is an asset to the entire city. A park's goals should include not only providing people with access to fresh air and nature for their recreation but also a place where they can meet and enjoy each other's company. Parks should promote pride in the community. Parks are for all people regardless of income, race, and sex because they are open to anyone who wishes to use them.

Ninety-nine percent of the urban parks in America are the typical park of low to moderate attendance, ordinary aesthetic value, and average maintenance. The remaining 1 percent are the parks that are truly outstanding—parks that are beautiful, have extremely high attendance, excellent maintenance, and are the ultimate asset to their city and its park department. What makes this 1 percent so special? Design! Management! People!

Park Design

During the mid-1800s, the American city park was a grand design of space and countryside, popularized by the Frederick Law Olmsted school of landscape architecture. Around the turn of the century, small neighborhood parks were developed that were designed to provide neighborhood playgrounds. Today, landscape architecture and park design face new challenges. Due to the growing number of urban Americans, the need for open space as envisioned by Olmsted is neither needed nor desired today. In fact, since the mid-1960s, neighborhood playgrounds have been experiencing a gradual renovation. Most urban residents want physical recreation facilities. They want attractive parks that also serve a purpose. While municipal governments are concerned with capital expenditures, operations, and maintenance of the parks, the park user is concerned with recreation programming and supervision, park hours, police protection, and lastly operation and maintenance. Today, parks in the city have to be as well designed as any building.

Meeting the demands of the park user as well as the municipal government can be a major challenge for the park designer. Careful design and attention to detail are his or her primary assets. Many beautiful designs can also be maintenance nightmares. Careful design begins with a site analysis of the park: what are its natural and cultural assets? What are its intended uses? Because there are so many factors to think about when designing a park, consider studying and researching each of the items in the following landscape survey.

Landscape Survey

Natural Features

A. **Vegetation:** Deciduous; coniferous; other types; virgin timber; existing and at time of settlement; stumpage value; biotic value; crops; ecology; plant lists; and density.

B. **Geology:** Geological cycle; formations; mineral deposits and extractions; rocks; outcrops; bedrock depth; soils; gravel deposits and extractions; drainage; erosion by wind, water, or ice; atmosphere; and borings.

C. **Geomorphology:** Topography; contours; high; low; slopes; artificial; caves; and views—good and bad.

D. **Hydrology:** Water; watersheds; flood plains; levels; changes; test analysis; streams; lakes; rivers; oceans; swamps; aquifers; tides; and tidal fluctuations.

E. **Climate:** Wind direction and speed; precipitation—rain, snow, hail, sleet, fog, mist, humidity; accumulation; temperature; degree days; sun and shade; solar radiation; intensity; daylight; inclination; sun and frost pockets; hurricanes; and micro/macroclimate.

F. **Wildlife:** Birds; fish; animals; wild; domestic; agrarian; sanctuaries; introductions; facing extinction; economic importance; and nuisances.

Cultural Features

G. **Transportation:** Trails—foot, bridle, snowmobile; roads; railroads; shipping; harbors and marinas; airports and flight paths; traffic volume; history and projections; proximity; facilities available; and entry and exit to the site.

H. **Community facilities:** Schools; churches; industry; historical sites and buildings; cemeteries; landmarks; archaeological sites; architecture; neighboring influences; ownership and acquisition; site expansion; character; type; texture; natural beauty; usable areas; and physical treatment.

I. **Utilities:** Overhead—lines and poles; underground—sewers, water, gas; underground pipelines—oil and gas; and availability.

J. **Controlling agencies:** Federal; state; local; planning; zoning; health; and other constraints—deeds, restrictions, covenants, permits, leases, acquisitions.

K. **Uses:** Past use; present use; residential; rural; agriculture; recreation; industrial; and others.

L. **Pollution:** Dumps, garbage; junk; air—smog; water and sewage; noise; and odors.

M. **Economics:** Minerals; lumber and forest products; agriculture; hunting; trapping; fishing; other commercial; resources of site and its surroundings; advertising; and tourism.

N. **Required needs:** Recreation; expansion of present uses; preservation; restoration; renovation; and conservation.

O. **Other studies:** Recreation; population; similar out-of-state studies; and design criteria.

After careful and complete research, all of the above features can be analyzed for their relative importance for the planned park, and for the interrelationships among those features that apply to the site being studied.

The park designer must also think about what the park's purpose will be. Does it provide an oasis from the urban landscape? Does it have historical significance? Is it a focal point for activities? Does it encourage community spirit and involvement? Does it have a special function? Due consideration must be given to aesthetics, function, and the interrelationships among all the elements. Careful analysis of both the site and its intended uses will usually result in diagrams that relate one use to another, with each use assigned to an appropriate site within the park. This will clearly define the uses and functions of the public open space.

With the diagram of uses and an analysis of the site's natural features and uses, a land use plan can be created. The more attention given to the plan, the better the design will be and the greater the likelihood of success. Attention should also be given to details such as site amenities, furniture, pavements, plant selection, and standard details for construction. These latter include items such as detailed cross sections, proper planting details, special requirements and needs, and so on. Don't forget safety and handicap accessibility either. Also consider how plants can be used to enhance the site, its positive features and its architectural purposes.

Management

If a park is to be successful, management must be one of the primary considerations, for it will be needed in abundance. Funding should be more than adequate to ensure that the pristine glory of the park's origin is preserved and enhanced. The most successful parks have separate funding or trust funds so management is never withheld and funding is never an issue.

Management begins with a plan and ends with people. The plan must show all the areas within the park as well as the amount and quality of maintenance required. The plan should also show the amount of maintenance required for each section of each park. For example, all areas needing weekly mowing should be outlined; the areas needing large mowers can also be keyed to the plan, with all the leftover areas representing trimming mower areas. All areas needing optimum turf or shrub care can also be noted, all pest control areas can be shown, and so on. In short, plans indicate what has to be done and where. A plan's maps will also show the work crews where their assignments will be and can be sorted into maintenance zones to improve maintenance efficiency throughout the parks in the city or park district.

An inventory and evaluation of the workforce, its positions and qualifications as well as all of the equipment and the condition of each tool is also essential. This will provide for maximum personnel and equipment efficiency and distribution. Several sections of this book will expand on the key points of management outlined here.

People

Involved people are one of the most important features of a successful park. For example, all the people potentially affected by the park need to be present during the design stage so all their concerns can be addressed. Likewise, during the fundraising campaigns experienced professionals need to be available to ensure that the best products available are used and that funds for a management program are allocated and maintained.

Urban residents are becoming more vocal and are demanding a part in the planning, construction, and maintenance of their environment. Reflecting this, the National League of Cities now advocates greater citizen participation in park and recreation planning. Residents want parks where people can go to be neighborly, enjoy natural beauty, and take advantage of new, safe equipment for their children. Parents also want park security. Nevertheless, most professional consultants, municipal leaders, and government agencies agree that current levels of community participation are still not high enough. Everyone needs to encourage more participation from their neighbors and leaders. Park development projects are magnets for the city as a whole as well as for their neighborhoods, and they can bring everyone together.

The urban park user is very class conscious. Middle-class recreation programs and their staff members, for example, will not be acceptable for inner city parks, and the urban park should accordingly be acquired or remodeled according to local citizen demands. Public neighborhood meetings, with the park planner as a leader, should be the instrument for determining the recreation facilities required as well as the means for providing them. Local residents should be encouraged to build the facilities and then to provide the leaders to operate the programs. Local residents should be involved in the park's management programs as well. Local pride in a park comes from participating in its development and making the decisions that lead to its construction.

Successful Parks: Boston's Post Office Square Park

The best way to illustrate the importance of the design, management, and people principles just outlined is by example. An outstanding example of a successful park is Post Office Square Park in the heart of Boston's financial district. This 1.7-acre park has been described as "The perfect park in a perfect location, with a perfect design and having perfect maintenance," and it stands as one of the great public improvements in the history of the city of Boston.

Originally, the site contained a small municipal park (see Fig. 1.1) and a two-story municipal parking garage dating from the 1950s that was falling apart. A group of 20 firms and individuals formed the Friends of Post Office Square in 1983 and they hired the best architectural, engineering, and landscape architectural firms they could afford. With plans in hand, they raised money. They got control of the garage from the city and demolished it. They then built a six-level underground garage and built the park on the top level, which was also at street level. The entire process took 11 years to complete from the design stage to project completion. The park contains marvelous green English glass and bronze fountains (see Fig. 1.2), which children play in on weekends; a small outdoor cafe; a lawn for picnickers (see Fig. 1.3) and sunbathers; gardens containing 125 species of trees, shrubs, and flowers (see Fig. 1.4); and seven varieties of vines on the trellis, which is studded with thousands of small lights. All the park's gardens grow in 4 feet of rich topsoil and many of the specimen plants have been loaned to the park by the Arnold Arboretum (which found itself with a great many trees and shrubs that had unknown parentage or were not true to species but which, because they were gifts, could only be disposed of through loans).

The Post Office Square Park provides a focal point for Boston's financial district (see Fig. 1.5), and buildings around the park have oriented them-

Fig. 1.1

Fig. 1.2

Fig. 1.3

Fig. 1.4

selves toward the park like campers to a bonfire. The plantings invite visitors to the park, which exists as a green space that feels whole and unthreatened. The lawn has a shape of its own and acts as a design element in its own right. It is not the "leftover" space or a means of passage through the park, despite the fact that the park's parking garage delivers over 1000 people a day through the park. The public rest rooms are clean 24 hours a day, and great attention has been given to the smallest details. Maintenance, provided by partial receipts from the garage's 1400 parking spaces, is abundant (the remaining receipts are given to the city). During the first year of operation, the park received 16 awards for excellence in design, and the entire park is a smooth-operating, well-managed, and beautiful facility.

The key element in the park's success was the original goal of the Friends to *make* it a success. They raised sufficient funds to hire the best design firms available and provided the energy to make the project work. They were the leaders and provided the inspiration. They held public hearings to ensure the proper mix of park uses and to meet the desires of the neighborhood, even though that neighborhood was transient, with only daytime users. Moreover, the Friends made sure the park would always have sufficient income to allow for a large professional management staff. Long after the park was completed the Friends still meet to make the improvements necessary for the park's continuing success.

Picnic Areas

Successful parks have many components. One element usually required by all parks is the provision of food for the park user. Boston's Post Office Square Park, for example, has a small cafe. Most U.S. parks, however, provide simpler food services such as a nearby concession or restaurant or a picnic table or two. Picnic areas are usually found in parks' wooded areas and are associated with playgrounds, open space, ball fields, comfort facilities, and parking lots.

Fig. 1.5

Pine needles and the leaves on the forest floor are the best ground cover for picnic areas. If grass is to be maintained, however, trees should be far enough apart to accommodate mowing equipment and allow sunlight to reach the grass. High trimming of branches and the placement of mulch at the base of the trees will protect the trees, permit grass growth, and create a very shady atmosphere. A minimum of 40 percent of the total area must be in sun at any one time, although 60 percent is more desirable for proper grass growth. Care should also be given to preventing compaction of the soil, which will cause the trees to decline. The installation of permanent paved pads for the picnic tables and walks to the pads will help minimize soil compaction, but care must be taken in the design so the paths are located where people want to walk. One successful park installed its walks a year after its completion so the paths could be installed where visitors had already made trails.

Over the winter, the park's tables should be repaired. If the picnic area is subject to floods, the tables should be stacked up and cabled together in the stacked position. A few tables and barrels should be left for the last fall and first spring picnickers, however, especially in a public park.

Garbage and trash removal can be improved by providing recycling trash barrels so park users will sort their trash into paper, cans and bottles, and unsorted trash. Trash pickup is improved by using the latest in garbage packer or recycling vehicles. The trash containers should be near groups of picnic tables (see Fig. 1.6) and close to the road or parking area to provide easy access for the packer. Trash pickup in parks is usually required only on a Monday or Friday, although the maintenance leader's experience will indicate when the containers will need attention. All trash receptacles should be kept as clean and neat as possible to present the appearance of good maintenance and to discourage misuse.

When abuse such as residents dumping household trash into a public barrel is detected, the park employee who empties the trash should sort through it to find

Fig. 1.6

mail showing the address of the person doing the dumping. That resident can then be sent a letter explaining that dumping is considered littering and that household trash should be properly disposed of. The letter should explain where the trash should go as well as the penalty for continued abuse of the public barrel. A record of these letters should be kept so second offenses can be dealt with accordingly. Enforcement by the local courts will work very well to stop dumping from recurring, and where this has been done, experience shows that the incidents of dumping have been cut in half after a few years of enforcement.

Successful Parks: Aberdeen's Wylie Park

Wylie Park in Aberdeen, South Dakota, is another example of a successful park. It was purchased by this city of 30,000 in 1910 and today covers 210 acres. By 1916, the park had expanded, and some buffalo and wildlife exhibits of animals and birds that are native to the north central United States were set up and today are still popular attractions. The following year brought a large pavilion that has been used for picnics, meetings, weddings, family reunions, Saturday night dances, a Lawrence Welk concert, and other special events. Today, the pavilion is on the National Register of Historical Places. A lake was built in 1920, which continues to be a popular venue for swimming and fishing. Every year it is stocked for the children (up to age 16) who are allowed to fish there.

A major change occurred to Wylie Park in 1971 when a children's theme park called Storybook Land (see Fig. 1.7) began development. This park within a park, developed primarily through donations, features fairy tales and nursery rhyme amusements. Some of its more unique contributions include the brick house built by a local mason for the "Three Little Pigs" display, with statues provided by the Mid-Dakota Pork Producers; the "Piggy Bank," provided by the same association, designed to encourage visitors' donations; the knights around the castle (see Fig. 1.8), each donated by the local Knights of Columbus; and an antique fire engine restored and provided by the city's fire department (see Fig. 1.9). Jack and Jill's hill, complete with a well, (see Fig. 1.10) was built to provide views of the park, and the hill acts as a ride for children, who can slide or roll down from its top. Other unique gifts include "The House that Jack Built," constructed by a local contractor; a lion drinking fountain from the local Lion's Club; a miniature horse feature donated by a local Shriner's horse patrol and a second horse given by a local saddle club; "Paul Bunyon," from the Modern Woodmen of America Camp, and "Babe the Blue Ox," donated by the local lumber company's employees; and "Little Miss Muffet"—eating her curds and whey—provided by The Food Bonanza. In 1985, a $250,000 castle was built with donations from residents who purchased engraved bricks. Figure 1.11 illustrates how the castle is used for functions (its concessionaire is shown at the left side of the photo). On the right side of the castle is a stage, and the engraved bricks surround the fountain.

Other features of Storybook Land include "Mary, Mary Quite Contrary," tending her garden (Fig. 1.12) with "Jack's Beanstalk" in the background; "Hickory,

Fig. 1.7

Fig. 1.8

Dickory, Dock and Mouse," which features a slide house (shown in Fig. 1.13), and "The Troll" and "Billy Goat Gruff" (shown in Fig. 1.14); the "Cow Jumping over the Moon" (Fig. 1.15), located right outside the gift shop concession; and "Yogi Bear with Boo Boo" (shown in Fig. 1.16).

The popularity of Wylie Park's Storybook Land led to the development of a second area called the Land of Oz, a theme selected because the author of *The Wizard of Oz*, L. Frank Baum, once lived and worked in Aberdeen. The project is expected to take seven to ten years to complete. Some of its features, such as the "Tin-Man," have been donated by a local scrap metal recycling company. All the characters are shown in Fig. 1.17, and the rainbow entrance is illustrated in Fig. 1.18.

Fig. 1.9

Fig. 1.10

Fig. 1.11

Fig. 1.12

Fig. 1.13

Fig. 1.14

The popularity of this park is so high that visitor demand often exceeds the facility's capacity. In 1986, municipal efforts led to improvements to the facility. A city sewer was brought in to serve all the buildings, the picnic area was doubled in size with additional shelters and new recreation facilities, a larger beach was built, the zoo and wildlife exhibits were enlarged, camping facilities were increased from 16 to 48 sites, 3 miles of trails were built, and the parking lots were expanded. All of

Fig. 1.15

Fig. 1.16

Fig. 1.17

Fig. 1.18

these improvements were paid for through a 1-percent city sales tax. Picnic shelter rentals, campground fees, concessions, and other special lease arrangements covered the costs of such improvements as a waterslide, a concession building, miniature golf course, and a rollerblade and bicycle rental. The park continues to be successful because it continues to change with the times, and the Aberdeen Parks, Recreation, and Forestry Board ensures that the park is properly maintained and adequately funded. Because its recreational opportunities are as important as its tourism value, Wylie Park makes an important contribution to the citizens of Aberdeen.

References

"A Winning Park," *American City & County*, December 1993: 26–29.

Campbell, Robert, "Post Office Square: The Perfect Park," *Boston Globe*, July 24, 1992: 17.

"Storybook Land," *City Trees*, November/December 1992: 5.

Note

Special thanks to Dan Ostrander, City Forester in Aberdeen, South Dakota, for supplying background information about Wylie Park.

2 🌿

Playground Design

While playgrounds are sometimes a part of a park, they can also comprise the entire site. The development of a successful playground begins with a proper design, which must address many features, especially those dealing with the needs of children and the physically challenged. Some typical requirements include gentle slopes, good site drainage, an absence of steps except on equipment, variations in the level of challenge offered by the equipment, and, above all, safety.

Playgrounds provide a variety of learning and play environments. The elements of the playground are described below and illustrated in Fig. 2.1.

1. **Entrances** provide information and social contact points, and accessibility is important.

2. **Pathways** provide access for children and wheeled vehicles such as toy cars, wheelchairs, baby carriages, and bikes. They should have firm surfaces and gentle 1:12 slope (1-foot rise for every 12 feet of length) maximum grade. They should be a minimum of 5 feet wide, and any sloped area should extend no longer than 12 feet before a level rest area or landing is provided. The design and layout can create different experiences for the user. The route must have protective surfacing to prevent injuries yet be firm enough to allow easy rolling for the small wheels of a wheelchair. At the equipment end of the entrance path, a 3-x-4-foot wheelchair parking space should be provided at the transfer point. Grab bars on the equipment will enable the children to get out of their chairs and onto the structure. There should not be any steps on an outdoor walkway without a nearby wheelchair ramp. Any steps on the playground equipment can be no higher than 8 inches and must be 12 inches deep and 24

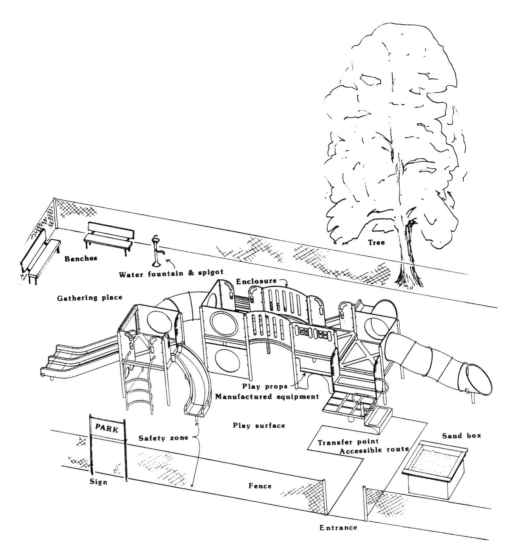

Fig. 2.1

inches wide. A series of steps should be close by any slides so handicapped children can hitch themselves back up the structure or return to their chairs.

3. **Signs** can be informative and playful. They should be a part of the walls, floors, structures, ceilings, and roof lines and should indicate that everyone is welcome.

4. **Enclosures** define a child's play environment. The enclosure should be accessible and in no way harmful to the children.

5. **Fences and barriers** protect the playground from abuse and overuse and are often used to keep the children from wandering outside the grounds.

6. **Manufactured equipment** has the greatest play value. Such equipment should be safe, meet current standards, and be easily maintained. Playground equipment comes in different types of wood as well as in steel, aluminum, plastic, and combinations of these materials. At a minimum, the equipment should have decks, grab bars, rails, slides, and swings. If playground equipment is to be built, it should not be homemade. Such equipment can easily be improperly and unsafely designed by well-meaning but uninformed individuals. Only manufactured equipment provides the safety and design liability for municipal equipment, and all equipment must meet the requirements of the U.S. Consumer Product Safety Commission's (CPSC) 1991 guidelines, the 1993 standards from the American Society for Testing and Materials (ASTM), and the Americans with Disabilities Act of 1990 (ADA). All hardware must be stainless steel or hot-dipped galvanized steel with all exposed bolts capped. All plastic must be UV-resistant, flame-retardant, and rotationally molded. All woods must be decay-resistant and No. 1 grade, with no splinters and only rounded edges. If volunteers are available, they should be used to raise funds to purchase equipment and, if desired, to assist with the assembly of the manufactured equipment. Do not use volunteers to build a playground by themselves!

   The playground designer might also want to be sure all the components are politically or environmentally correct. The specifications could require wood, for example, that does not come from old-growth forests. All timber plots should be replanted. The wood preservative treatment process should occur after the wood has been cut to size for the playground. This ensures that the waste wood can be recycled into particle boards. All steel and aluminum components should be made from recycled material. If sand is used as a mold in the casting operations, it too should be recycled. All paint should be powder-coated so there is no lead and no aerosol sprays are used. The shipping crate should be made of recycled lumber and a maximum amount of recycled cardboard. If styrofoam peanuts are used, they should be made of the biodegradable starch type. The playground surface should be made of untreated natural wood fiber mulch or recycled rubber.

7. **Play surfaces** are the soft cushioned surfaces surrounding the equipment. Natural surfaces are those areas outside of the play surface. Play surfaces should meet CPSC guidelines to protect children and to prevent serious injury in falls. Natural surfaces belong outside the safety zone around the equipment, which extends approximately 6 feet from the equipment. However, the zone will vary in size depending on the equipment and the manufacturer's recommendations. There are several new codes that deal with the provision of a resilient surface under all equipment in locations where children might fall and be injured. These codes must be followed even if existing surfaces have to be changed.

   There are several considerations that should be evaluated when selecting a play surface material. These include installation and purchase cost, long-term maintenance cost, permanence, containment needs, good footing, safety from falls, appearance, vandalism potential, flammability, and drainage. More features of play surfaces are discussed in the next chapter on playground safety.

8. **Game areas** support the development of athletic skill, cooperation, and large-muscle control as well as the learning of the rules of various sports.

9. **Landforms and topographic changes** help children explore movement and increase circulation. The games children play on landforms might include hide-and-seek, rolling, climbing, sliding, and jumping, which stimulate orientation and perception skills. At Aberdeen, South Dakota's Wylie Park, for example, a hill with a long slide was built to provide children with a play area for precisely these activities.

10. **Water** is used for play in many different ways. Its multisensory impact makes a substantial contribution to childrens' development.

11. **Sand** is another universal play material. Sandboxes allow for the development of children's imagination and social interaction skills. Because sandboxes attract children of all ages, they should be readily accessible.

12. **Play props** comprise the things children like to play with, such as sticks, stones, scraps, lumber, dress-up clothes, bikes, and the like. Many features on common playground equipment, such as steering wheels, store fronts, and so on, also function as play props.

13. **A gathering place** to support social development and cooperation is important for children as well as for the adults who socialize while supervising them. Adults need comfortable places for sitting, and accessibility is very important. Facilities for supervision by adults as well as park facilities such as picnicking areas, benches, trees, trash receptacles, and water accommodations should be located near the equipment.

14. **Stage settings** support performance activities, which encourage self-esteem and teamwork. Stage performances also foster a sense of community and promote local culture.

15. **A field house** is desirable for rest rooms, communication centers, emergency facilities, and the storage of equipment.

16. **Trees** and other plants are enjoyed for their beauty and their shade. Gardens promote learning about plants and interaction with nature. These areas should be made accessible.

17. **Animals,** whether wild or domestic, stimulate caring and the development of responsibility toward other living things. Play areas can provide an opportunity to observe nature.

Remember that not all of these elements are required for a playground to be successful.

Successful Playgrounds: Wellesley's Warren Park

The Warren Park playground, recently rebuilt in Wellesley, Massachusetts, provides an example of a successful playground facility. It sits on the site of a former school playground, which, when the school closed and was converted to other

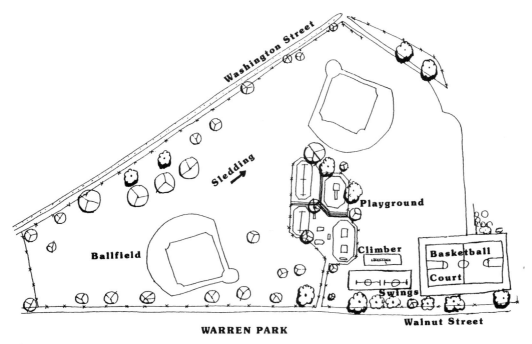

Washington Street

Sledding

Playground

Ballfield

Climber

Basketball

Court

Swings

Walnut Street

WARREN PARK

Fig. 2.2

uses, sat idle except for occasional use by neighborhood children. Figure 2.2 shows the playground, located in the center of the park as a whole. (The school building is just off the plan, on the right.)

In the early spring of 1990, a group of neighborhood parents got together to form the Friends of Warren Park and to work with Wellesley's landscape architect to master plan a new playground for the site. The first phase of the planning process consisted of developing a plan for the entire property that was acceptable to everyone and provided a total play experience. The plan located open areas, baseball fields, a basketball court, a playground, and the components of the playground equipment as well as preserving the park's trees and flower beds. It also avoided all conflicts with utilities and other long-term problems for the site. The group met two weeks later to approve the plan and to decide on which pieces of playground equipment to purchase, how the equipment should be arranged, and how funds could be raised to build the project. The playground equipment was designed for preschool activities in one area and 5-to-12-year-old activities in another (see Fig. 2.3). Both areas provided for all types of activity, from coordination and play value to balance and strength activities such as running, climbing, sliding, swinging, and using arms and legs. It was decided that the funding would be 60 percent from municipal sources and 40 percent from the neighborhood. In addition, the neighborhood would provide the labor to help assemble the equipment and build the timber-retaining walls required because the playground was built on a slope.

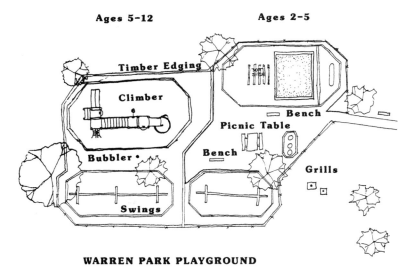

WARREN PARK PLAYGROUND

Fig. 2.3

By early summer, construction was well underway, and the neighbors began painting the old school equipment that was to be saved, relocated, or rehabilitated. They built timber walls and edging or headers around the four components of playground equipment (see Fig. 2.4) that were to contain the playground surfacing material. After the new equipment was installed (see Fig. 2.5), the play surface was added, the entire area was cleaned up, and the area outside the equipment areas was loamed and seeded. Half of the area was resurfaced for carriage and stroller accessibility and to provide a location for new benches, picnic tables, a charcoal grill, and a water bubbler. Three swings were replaced with infant seats, and in August a neighborhood picnic was held to celebrate the completion of the project (see Fig. 2.6). Figure 2.7, a photograph taken during the celebration, shows the cake that was decorated to recreate the equipment shown in Fig. 2.5.

It was at this point, however, that the real change occurred. The novelty of new equipment and a new playground did not wear off. In fact, as the weeks went by Warren Park became "the place to go," and people came from all over the community as well as from surrounding cities. The following spring, a survey was conducted to determine why the park had become so popular. It was found that a major factor was that the playground was highly visible from two main roads, and the site also contained several large shade trees. People driving by could see children having a great time, and this encouraged them to stop. Moreover, the entire site is aesthetically pleasing and inviting, with the bright colors of the equipment blending harmoniously with the timber edging and wood-chipped areas.

Although public participation in the construction may have been a factor in the park's popularity, it was not the sole reason—many other playgrounds built with neighborhood help have not been as successful as Warren Park. Neither was visibility necessarily a primary reason for success, as other playgrounds

Fig. 2.4

Fig. 2.5

Fig. 2.6

Fig. 2.7

in Wellesley are even more visible but not nearly as popular. The safety of the playground and its equipment also contributed to the park's success. The surface treatment for cushioning falls was a major success factor because of the number of parents who brought their children to the park to play. In addition, age groups were separated by timber enclosures so toddlers couldn't wander accidentally into the areas set aside for older children, and the equipment was purchased from a company with an excellent safety record as well as a reputation for products that are easy to maintain. The site's amenities, from picnic tables and grills to water facilities and carriage access, also contributed to the park's popularity.

But the biggest factor in Warren Park's success was the welcome the neighborhood adults gave to visiting adults who brought their children to the playground. Because of the way the area is designed, adults can easily watch their children while talking to adults whose interests, ages, and children's ages mirror their own. In fact, considerable effort was expended in designing the site to make it inviting for the adults.

In the years that followed the completion of the Warren Park playground, the Friends have continued to meet and expand on their success. The ball fields were renovated and repaired to make them more usable for neighborhood children. Fund-raising efforts promoted the construction of a basketball court and three large structures for children over 8 years old, and plans were in the works for additional equipment designed for teenagers. The site was also modified to make it handicap-accessible.

Warren Park's playground has experienced only one incident of vandalism, and it was very minor. Its success continues to grow, and greater pride in the playground and community has been the result.

Accessibility for the Disabled

On January 26, 1992, Title II of the ADA of 1990 became effective. The ADA prohibits any form of discrimination because of disability. The act encompasses accommodations at parks, zoos, recreation areas, schools, gyms, and the like, while expanding on and clarifying section 504 of the Rehabilitation Act of 1973. The CPSC's guidelines, the ASTM's standards, and the ADA have a major impact on the design and development of America's public playgrounds. In particular, the ADA specifically requires that "each service, program, or activity conducted by a public entity . . . be readily accessible to, and usable by, individuals with disabilities . . . except where to do so would result in a fundamental alteration in the nature of the program or in undue financial and administrative burdens." The law covers "both indoor and outdoor areas where human constructed improvements, structures, equipment, or property have been added to the natural environment." Any individual or group can file a complaint charging discrimination on the basis of disability. The Department of Interior is responsible for administering the law as it relates to parks and recreation areas.

Park and playground designers and operators must make all necessary changes to existing playgrounds as well as new areas to accommodate the disabled. Accessibility does not mean that every part of every playground should be available to every child but that some components and play experiences must be available to handicapped children. Playgrounds must also provide access to all handicaps—not just those that confine children to wheelchairs. Accommodations must be made for the visually, mentally, and hearing impaired. Examples of playground features for all handicapped children might include fragrant flowers for the blind, wind chimes for the mentally handicapped, and wildlife observations for the deaf.

Safety on playgrounds should not be compromised for the sake of accessibility. Items required for accessibility—such as larger decks, shorter heights for steps, and more railings, ramps, and grab bars—will also make the structure safer and more enjoyable for all the children using it. Making a playground accessible does not mean it will be successful, usable, or safe. A successful playground, however, is always accessible, usable, and safe.

References

"Choosing an Environmentally Correct Playground," *American City & County*, October 1993, p. 11.

McIntyre, Sally, "How Many Parks Make a Playground," *Parks & Recreation*, March 1987, p. 27–29.

3

Playground Safety

Playground safety in the United States falls under two sets of standards: the U.S. Consumer Product Safety Commission (CPSC) guidelines and the American Society for Testing and Materials (ASTM) standards. The CPSC is an independent regulatory agency of the federal government whose responsibility is to inform the public of unreasonable risks associated with consumer products. In 1981, the Commission published the *Handbook for Public Playground Safety*, consisting of general guidelines directed at playgrounds for children aged 5 to 12. In 1991, the ASTM published a new set of guidelines that included recommendations for equipment designed for 2-to-5-year-olds and 5-to-12-year-olds. Although not a mandatory standard, this federal document has been viewed as a benchmark for the design of safe playground equipment. The ASTM is a scientific and technical organization with voluntary consensus standards. In 1993, the ASTM set up a group to develop safety standards for playground equipment that published its findings in a document called *ASTM Standard F1487-93*.

The following standards are taken from the CPSC's *Handbook for Public Playground Safety:*

1. **Age:** "age-appropriate playground designs should accommodate [children] with regard to the type, scale, and the layout of equipment; 'preschool' refers to children 2 to 5 years old, and 'school-age' refers to children 5 to 12 years old. . . . In playgrounds intended to serve children of all ages the layout of pathways and the landscaping of the playground should show the two distinct areas for the two age groups. . . . Signs posted in the playground area can

be used to give some guidance to adults as to the age appropriateness of the equipment."

2. **Entrapment:** "An opening may present an entrapment hazard [where children could get stuck or injured] if the [hole] between any [two] surfaces is [between] 3.5 inches [and] 9 inches."

3. **Guardrails and Protective Barriers:** Guardrails are rails with openings more than 9 inches apart while protective barriers eliminate any possibility of passage. On preschool equipment, guardrails can be used on equipment up to 30 inches high, and protective barriers are required for equipment over 30 inches in height. On school-age equipment, guardrails can be used for equipment up to 48 inches high, but stepped platforms are preferred. Protective barriers are necessary on equipment more than 48 inches high.

4. **Steps:** "the maximum difference in height between stepped platforms should be:

   Preschool Age Children (2–5 years): 12 inches

   School-Age Children (5–12 years): 18 inches

   The space between the stepped platforms should be closed if the space exceeds 9 inches."

5. **Slides:** "in case of a freestanding slide, it is recommended that the platform [at the top] have a minimum length of at least 22 inches. At the entrance to the chute there should be a means to channel the user into a sitting position. Slides with flat open chutes should have sides with a 4 inch minimum height. The exit region should be essentially horizontal and have a minimum length of 11 inches. Roller slides are not recommended for public playgrounds unless frequent maintenance can be guaranteed."

6. **Swings:** "it is recommended that no more than two single swings be hung in each bay of the supporting structure. Attaching swings to composite structures is not recommended. The minimum clearance between the seating surface of a tire swing and the uprights of the supporting structure should be 30 inches when the tire is in a position closest to the support structure." The distance between two swing seats should be no less than 24 inches when hanging at rest.

7. **Surfaces:** "The surfacing material used under and around . . . equipment should have a Critical Height value . . . of the highest accessible part of the equipment." Bare metal surfaces on slides and equipment should be avoided not only for safety reasons but because of the high temperatures such surfaces can reach when exposed to prolonged sunlight.

   Figure (3.1) below summarizes the allowable heights of equipment as they relate to the depth and type of surfacing:

8. **Safety Zone:** The area covered with protective surfacing includes all areas under and around the equipment as well as 6 feet from all equipment. Cer-

Fig. 3.1 Critical Heights of Playground Surface Materials (heights in feet)

Material	Depth of Material			
	6 inch	9 inch	12 inch	Compressed 9 inch
Wood mulch	7	10	11	10
Shredded bark	6	10	11	7
Uniform wood chips	6	7	12	6
Fine sand	5	5	9	5
Coarse sand	5	5	6	4
Fine gravel	6	7	10	6
Medium gravel	5	5	6	5
Poured-in-place rubber	23	(1⅝″–4′)	(2⅛″–7′)	(2⅜″–8′)
Rubber safety surface tiles	15	(1¾″–4 to 7′)	(2½″–6 to 12′)	(3″–9 to 14′)

Note: The rubber tiles vary depending upon the manufacturer's design and material. Check with the manufacturer for specific safety requirements for each rubber product. Much of the information in Fig. 3.1 is derived from the *Handbook for Public Playground Safety*.

tain pieces of equipment such as swings and slides require a safety zone of 6 feet or more.

9. **Sharp Edges:** There should be no sharp edges, points, or corners that could puncture skin.

10. **Protrusions:** Projections and protrusions that could entangle clothing are prohibited.

11. **Pinch Points:** There should be no points or closing angles that could entrap clothing or body parts. There should be no loose fastenings.

12. **Tripping Hazards:** All anchors and bars that could trip running children should be below the playing surface. Likewise, suspended hazards in high-traffic areas must be visible or more than 7 feet above the surface.

13. **Sliding Poles:** Poles should be at least 38 inches higher than and 18 to 20 inches away from the deck they are attached to. The pipe diameter should be 1.9 inches or less.

14. **Horizontal Ladders:** The distance between rungs should not exceed 15 inches, and the first rung should not be directly over the platform or climbing rungs.

Additional information and illustrations clarifying these standards can be obtained from the CPSC's *Handbook,* the *ASTM Standard F1487-93,* and the ADA guidelines.

Accidents on playgrounds are a major concern for any park superintendent. More than 120,000 serious accidents and an average of 17 deaths are reported on public playgrounds in the United States every year, and 60 percent of these involve children under 6 years of age. Lack of supervision and improper maintenance are causes of approximately one third of these accidents. To address these concerns, the ASTM standard defines maintenance specifications. In order to prevent accidents and legal suits of negligence, those responsible for maintenance must develop a preventative maintenance program in which inspections are frequent and the environmental characteristics of each playground are evaluated. A typical playground inspection form is shown in Fig. 3.2, and most playground manufacturers also have their own inspection sheets, which must be modified to meet local requirements.

Each inspection checklist should be attached to a plan (see Fig. 3.3) showing all of the playground's components. The plan should show the name of the equipment manufacturer, each separate component structure, and all the structures within the playground area. Such information is useful in tracking long-term maintenance needs and if necessary sources of replacement parts as well as in determining which components work well and which do not. If more than one manufacturer is represented within the same municipality, comparisons can be very useful in establishing a history of equipment durability.

All playgrounds must be inspected frequently. New equipment should be checked for entrapment areas, exposed footings or anchors, proper depth of the surfacing material, bare metal and trip hazards, protruding bolts or pipes, the absence of barriers between play areas, and neighboring dangers or hazards. The following components should be checked daily: "S" hooks, anchor bolts, guardrails and handrails, unplugged holes, and inspectors should look for sharp edges and points; missing or loose bolts; loose, worn, cracked, or broken pieces; surfaces under equipment; and broken welds. The following should be inspected weekly: exposed footings and worn bearings in addition to all of the daily items. Monthly inspections are necessary on wood surfaces, worn clevises, worn swing seats, and all the daily and weekly items. Everything else should be thoroughly checked twice a year. After each playground inspection, the inspection results must be written down and dated to reduce the community's liability if an accident occurs and a lawsuit is filed.

The inspection record should also indicate who the inspector is. The inspector must be very careful and must be trained in equipment installation and maintenance. The same inspector should be used repeatedly so any long-term deterioration will be noticed. The inspector should take notes on all problems and hazards and should undertake corrections later. The checklist should also include the date when problems were corrected as well as the date of the inspection.

Most playground manufacturers have local sales representatives. Occasionally, the sales rep is also qualified to do playground safety inspections. Doing this periodically provides a critical review and check on the inspections made by the regular inspector. If the sales representative does the routine inspections, it might be desirable to have another sales rep provide the second opinion.

PLAYGROUND INSPECTIONS

LOCATION _____

DATE _____

INSPECTOR _____

ACTION COMPLETION DATE _____

YES NO

— — Visible cracks, bending, warping, rusting or breakage or excessive wear of any component or part.
   PART NAMES: _____

— — Deformation of open hooks, rings, links etc.
   LOCATION: _____

— — Worn swing hangers, "S hooks" or chains on swings.
   LOCATION: _____

— — Missing, worn, cracked, or jagged swing seats.
   LOCATION: _____

— — Broken supports/anchors.
   LOCATION: _____

— — Concrete footings exposed, cracked, loose in ground.
   LOCATION: _____

— — Sharp edges or points.
   LOCATION: _____

— — Exposed ends of pipe that should be covered by plugs or caps.
   LOCATION: _____

— — Protruding bolt ends that do not have smooth finished caps/covers.
   PART/LOCATION: _____

— — Loose, worn, or rusted bolts, nuts, and other fasteners.
   LOCATION: _____

— — Splintered wood.
   LOCATION: _____

— — Lack of lubrication on moving parts.
   LOCATION: _____

— — Worn or squeaky bearings.
   LOCATION: _____

— — Broken or missing rails, steps, rungs, seats.
   LOCATION: _____

— — Surfacing material worn or scattered.
   LOCATION: _____

— — Swing chain wrapped around horizontal swing beams.
   LOCATION: _____

— — Chipped or peeling paint.
   LOCATION: _____

— — Broken glass, trash, or foreign objects within or on play equipment.
   LOCATION: _____

— — Pinch or crush points (exposed mechanisms, junctures, or moving components).
   LOCATION: _____

— — Tripping hazards such as roots, rocks, or other environmental obstacles.
   HAZARD & LOCATION: _____

— — Poor drainage areas.
   LOCATION: _____

— — Loose, twisting climbing rungs.
   LOCATION: _____

COMMENTS: _____

_____

_____

_____

_____

_____

_____

_____

_____

_____

_____

_____

Fig. 3.2

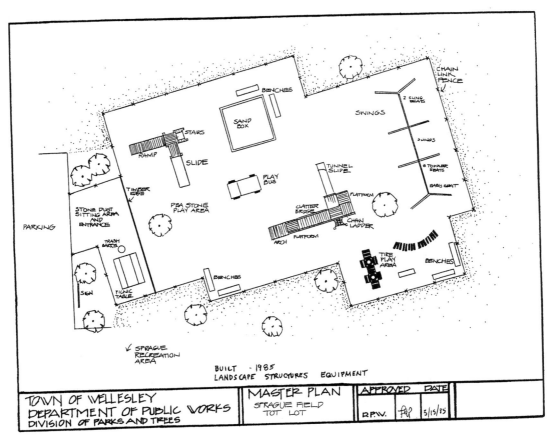

Fig. 3.3

References

King, Steven G., "Playground Accessibility Update," *Landscape Structures*, 1992.

U.S. Consumer Product Safety Commission, "Handbook for Public Playground Safety," Washington, D.C., 1991.

Wagner, Dan, vice president of Landscape Structures, Inc., Delano, MN, letter and inspection checklist, October 20, 1993.

4 Traffic Island Beautification

Besides parks and playgrounds, urban public open spaces can be beautified to make them attractive, easy to maintain, and a source of pride and beauty for any city. The beautification of a traffic island means a lot more than painting bituminous pavement a green color. Attractive landscaping in a traffic island not only draws immediate attraction to the island, it can provide an identity for an entire city, especially if all the city's traffic islands are landscaped.

Traffic island design is a study in contradictions. The driver's attention must not be diverted from traffic flow or directional signs, yet beautiful islands attract the driver's eye. Beautiful islands are a major asset to a community and a major source of appreciation for visitors driving through a city, but they can be troublesome to design and maintain.

Beautification can be achieved with such architectural treatments as the use of bricks, pavers, or other surface treatments as well as the use of raised planters, pedestrian shelters on a median island, and uniform signage structures. Beautification can also be accomplished with trees and low-maintenance shrubs, which can be supplemented with low-maintenance annuals and perennials. Beautification can also be as simple as a tree planting with mulch or turf areas. Turf areas, however, require frequent maintenance and because of the danger of crossing traffic to get to the island every week are not usually recommended.

Design

Once a traffic island has been selected for landscaping, a layout plan and site survey should be prepared. When curbing is desired, an engineer should be asked for the preferred layout of the new island. The engineer's main concerns are traffic flow first and beautification second. Despite the anticipated conflict between the two, this system works well: the engineer designs the layout and prepares a curb schedule, leaving the bulk of the site available for a landscape treatment. The planted island of a cul-de-sac will reduce the pavement by as much as 40 percent, reduce storm drainage by 30 percent, and improve the quality of the groundwater.

There are a few design rules to follow. The first is, the island should not be so busy visually as to divert the driver's attention and cause a traffic accident or so rigid that people might be injured if they hit something that doesn't move. This is particularly important when lights and signs become potential targets of vehicles out of control. All obstacles must have breakaway bolts to minimize injuries in an accident. Raised beds in a median, for example, must be designed to direct a vehicle back onto the highway. Trees and large shrubs are unforgiving in an accident, but they can be located behind a guardrail or median barrier. Native trees and seedlings that were preserved during construction are not subject to liability in the event of an accident, but trees planted after construction are, so the designer must keep this in mind when locating trees near highways and streets.

Another important rule to consider is simplicity in the design. The use of landscaping, for example, should consist of only two or three layers of plants: trees, shrubs, and ground covers (see Fig. 4.1). Within each of these layers, no more than three varieties of plants should be used. The simplest design of a traffic island or cul-de-sac might have a tree with five shrubs and fifteen ground covers around the tree, for a total of three separate varieties. A larger island or rotary might have a collection of three or more trees, surrounded by three varieties of shrubs and three varieties of perennials or ground covers. Some of the most attractive islands have a single specimen tree as a focal point, with masses of one or two varieties of perennials around the tree and a large percentage of the island covered with mulch. Raised centers of the island will enhance the height of the plant in the center and allow all the plants along the edge to be seen more easily, as illustrated in Fig. 4.2. If a view can be created through the island, it can greatly enhance its value.

Management

Low maintenance is another important rule of traffic island design. Low maintenance is necessary not only to save tax dollars, but more importantly to minimize the exposure to traffic by maintenance employees. Monthly visits to pull weeds has a lot less potential for creating accidents than weekly visits to mow grass. Low maintenance, however, does not mean low aesthetic value. There are a great number of trees, shrubs, groundcovers, annuals, and perennials that will look beautiful and still tolerate dust, dirt, exhaust fumes, winter salt, hazardous materials, and even being driven over periodically. Use these plants. Follow the recommenda-

Fig. 4.1

Fig. 4.2

tions for low-maintenance annuals and perennials listed in Appendix A of this book. Other books and publications also provide lists of these plants. Even local nursery catalogs are sources of information about what plants will survive in urban locations.

A study should be made to determine the cost effectiveness of beautified land-scapes. Select some relandscaped traffic islands and determine an annual mainte-nance labor-hour requirement before and after the beautification project occurred. The results of this study will show that a substantial percentage of the time spent maintaining traffic islands per year will be saved through such a program.

Traffic island maintenance is traditionally done by the highway or public works department that owns the street or highway. Sometimes, within a municipality, especially those with beautification programs, the city might have the park or tree department maintain the islands.

People

With the current trend toward using volunteers, many cities are putting their islands up for "adoption." This practice carries with it a great number of cautions, however. First of all, the municipality should continue to keep control over the planting design of the island. All of the guidelines outlined above should be followed, regardless of the funding source. Too many islands have a hundred varieties of annuals, for example, and show little concern for aesthetics. Other plant donations provided through traffic island adoption programs might have trees that will die or drop branches and fruit all over the street. Just because the plants are donated, the city does not have to accept poor taste or the wrong plants. Volunteers should receive safety vests and be cautioned about traffic and other hazards.

Signs that indicate the name of the plant's donor are somewhat controversial. Some say this is simply advertising necessary to obtain donors. However, an adequate number of donors will come forth if an article about them or the program appears in the local paper. Some say the display of the donor's name will eliminate poor maintenance during the growing season. However, this is also not always the case either. High maintenance standards have to be established by the city, and the volunteers will follow suit. When the volunteers lose interest, the city has to pitch in to help or take over. Keep in mind that volunteers do lose interest after a period of time. The city has to be prepared and may have to recruit new volunteers as often as once a year.

Fig. 4.3

Beautified traffic islands do add character to the municipality. Well-designed areas become more noticeable, and demand for beautification increases as more areas are beautified (see Fig. 4.3). Beautified islands will also increase the importance of the department responsible for the maintenance. The more visible and important your department becomes, the less effort is required to obtain reasonable funding and staff at budget allocation times.

References

Kendig, Lane H., and Cynthia Montague, "Landscaping Cul-de-Sacs" (centerfold), *NatureScape*, September 1981.

5 🌿

Parking Lots

Parking lots, like traffic islands, will set the tone and aesthetics for a city. Parking lots are either publicly or privately owned. Municipalities should require beautification for new, privately owned parking developments through the zoning process and should use its parking meter receipts to beautify the municipal lots (see Fig. 5.1). Beautified lots can be as simple as a few spaces on a vacant lot, with 10 percent of the property having landscaping, or as complicated as the parking garage at Boston's Post Office Square, where a park occupies the entire street level and there are six parking levels underground.

Design

Landscaping

Whether the parking lot is municipally owned or private, the same rules of design should apply. A typical zoning bylaw or ordinance pertaining to an off-street parking lot might contain the following landscape elements:

A. For an outdoor parking area containing 20 or more parking spaces, at least one tree should be planted for every 10 parking spaces on any side of the perimeter of the parking area.

B. In any outdoor parking area, a landscaped open space having a width of at least 5 ft and a depth equal to the adjacent parking space should be provided so that there are no more than 15 parking spaces in a continuous row. At least one tree should be planted and maintained in each open space.

Fig. 5.1

C. Trees should be at least 2 inches in diameter at the time of planting and should be a species with the appropriate suitability and hardiness for location in a parking lot.

Screening

Any parking area that abuts residential districts should be screened from them and from the street in accordance with the following requirements:

A. **Materials:** Plant materials characterized by dense growth that will form an effective year-round screen should be planted. To the extent practicable, existing trees should be retained and used.

B. **Height:** Screening should be at least 5 feet in height. When planted, plant materials should be no less than 3½ feet in height measured from the street grade. Lower plants should be used as a ground cover under a car's overhang. The low plants must be able to tolerate salt and exhaust. Grass should not be used here due to the obvious problems involved in mowing grass when cars are parked.

C. **Width:** Screening should be in a strip of landscaped open space at least 5 ft wide and located so as not to conflict with any corner visibility requirements.

D. **Maintenance:** All required plant materials should be maintained in a healthy condition and whenever necessary replaced with new plant materials to ensure continued compliance with screening requirements. All required fences and walls should be permanently maintained in good repair and presentable appearance, and whenever necessary they should be repaired or replaced.

E. **Lighting:** All artificial lighting used to illuminate a parking area should be arranged and shielded so as to prevent direct glare from the light source into any street or onto adjacent property.

Management Tips

Although not too much can be done to reduce parking lot maintenance, lines should be painted with plastic paint or tapes similar to those used on highways.

This eliminates expensive annual painting. Wheel stops or curbs should be used along the edges to prevent damage to any and all landscaping along the buffer as well as to eliminate the need for providing separate off-hours mowing under overhanging cars. Hedges and thorns might also be useful to control and direct pedestrian traffic through the parking lot. However, these same trees will catch and hold trash, so a wide variety of planting types and planting patterns should be provided within and along the borders of the lot.

References

Town of Wellesley zoning bylaw, Wellesley, Massachusetts, as amended 1977.

6

Trails, Bridges, and Retaining Walls

Most city parks need to provide variety for the park user in addition to aesthetic enjoyment. This chapter highlights some of the miscellaneous amenities that give a park its character, including trails, bridges, retaining walls, and pavers.

Trails

Park trails fall into five categories, each of which is discussed in the following paragraphs.

1. Woodland Paths

Design: Woodland paths can vary from wilderness trails that are seldom used, trails through meadows and prairies on packed-down grass (see Fig. 6.1), and woodland trails on packed-down leaves. Paths should be straight or have long curves to prevent shortcuts and abuse. Special treatment should be given to the park's noise generators so they will not offend other park users or abutting landowners. They should be less than 2 feet wide and designed for a single user.

Management: If the trail needs any maintenance at all, it is normally a spring cleanup to pick up winter damage or to ensure that the path is visible and the trails are all open. Some areas will require signs, blazes, or codes to mark the trail so hikers will not get lost. The most frequently used blaze is a blue dot along the trail going into the park and a yellow dot along the trail going out. Another type of blaze marking is a small metal tag indicating the trail's name and/or direction. Blazes should be located at every trail fork or major bend, and each blaze should

Fig. 6.1

be located at eyesight distance from the next. Woodland path trails are usually found in rural or wilderness areas, but sometimes large regional parks also have woodland trails.

Aside from trail surface maintenance, the most troublesome maintenance activity on any trail is the effort required to close those that have become undesirable. Once a new trail is discovered, the maintenance supervisor should act fast. It should be blocked with a log or stump to hide any trace of the trail. Waiting even a week's delay will cause the trail to become permanent and the construction of a major barricade will be a necessity. All trails should also be buffered with plant material to visually screen the trail user from other users or abutters to the park.

2. Gravel Trails

Design: Gravel trails are located in parks where foot traffic is moderate, where service and police access is necessary, and yet where aesthetics and focal points are very important. Gravel trails can be built with a base of gravel (see Fig. 6.2), stone, crushed rock, or sand and a surface layer of gravel, sand, wood chip (see Fig. 6.3), or mulch. These trails should average no more than 5 percent slope, but occasional steeper grades up to 12 percent are possible if the lengths are not too long. Gravel trails must be passable at all times of the year.

Management: Management of gravel trails consists of grading, correcting drainage, and replacing the surface layer as needed. Trails of this type are often found in small or suburban cities but are occasionally also found in large city parks where usage is low.

The bridle trail is a variation of the gravel trail. Bridle trails require excellent drainage to prevent mud puddles yet must be firm enough so horses will not loose their footing.

Motorbike trails are another variation. Motorbikes require a clay soil for the best traction, compaction, and wear tolerance. Motorbike trails require varied terrain and sight distance because occasional steep slopes and blind corners add interest and variety for the bike user. A level open area provides a place for the beginner to practice and become familiar with the bike. Low branches should be trimmed from trees nearest the trail. Cable gates and barbed wire should never be used in any park but especially not in areas where bikes are likely to be used.

Fig. 6.2

3. Paved Trails

Design: Paved trails carry the greatest number of users. Construction requires a good, well-drained base, and the surface can be bituminous (see Fig. 6.4), concrete, brick, or other hard surface. Paved trails are usually good for at least 20 years before a new surface is required. Construction costs for paved trails are the highest of all trail types. Paved trails are found in heavily used city parks.

The bicycle trail is a variation of the paved trail. Bike trails need to be a minimum of 6 feet wide, although 8 feet is preferable and 10 feet of headroom clearance is also necessary. A minimum shoulder of 3 feet is also necessary for recovery when bikes momentarily lose control. The shoulder can be grass or gravel. At intersections with streets, the bike trail needs to be ramped, like the handicap ramp and a crosswalk

Fig. 6.3

Fig. 6.4

marking used for pedestrians. The crosswalk also requires that signs be placed on the road to identify it as such. The trail should be marked into lanes for two-directional traffic. For safety reasons, there should not be any hairpin turns or turns at the bottom of a steep grade.

4. Sidewalks

Design: Any sidewalk or paved surface going through a city park requires certain minimum standards. The surface should be smooth, there should be no steps, and the material should be durable. The aesthetics of the surface material is of secondary importance, but it does add greatly to the overall impression of the park. Typical surfaces are concrete, bituminous asphalt, brick, concrete pavers, and stone materials, all of which require special installation methods to ensure longevity and a safe surface.

5. Stairways

Design: Although steps in public open spaces should be avoided because of the potential liability, there are some situations where stairs must be built. In these situations the stairs must be properly designed, built, and maintained, and above all, they must be safe. However, because stairs do not permit access by wheelchairs or carriages, alternative ramps are required.

The risers should be no more than 6 inches high. For comfort to the user, the formula for determining the height of risers is two times the riser height plus the width of the tread equals 26. When steps are used there should be a minimum of three risers. Stairways with more than 10 risers will need careful design to ensure adequate foundations and landings if necessary. Railings are necessary on each side of the stair at a height of 33 inches. If the number of people using the stairs in the evening is high, lights will be necessary. Figure 6.5 illustrates an excellent design found in a Chicago park.

Fig. 6.5

Bridges

1. Design: When possible, bridges should be designed with a clear span. This will eliminate high maintenance supports. Prefabricated clear span bridges can be built up to 400 feet in length if they are intended for pedestrians or light use. If steel or laminated wood beams are used, the clear span is a factor of the beam size. Prefabricated bridges have been engineered and can be purchased complete and ready to use. They are factory-built, trucked to the site, and lifted onto the foundation with a crane. There should be no steps on or leading to a bridge. Handrails should meet handicap and accessibility requirements. Turns and grades should be gentle. All bridges require strong foundations at each end. Most footbridges can be built with footings that go below the frost line and are large enough to support the bridge weight as well as the load weight. A structural engineer should be used for all bridge designs. Footbridges require a building permit so the local building inspector may have special requirements. Bridges over water will require environmental or wetlands permits as well.

One design tip that works well for small bridges is to drop the equivalent of one or two large inexpensive 2-by-4-by-4-foot concrete blocks (purchased surplus from a local concrete plant) into the excavated pit for the footing. Crushed stone or gravel provides an easily moved base for the block, and after the bridge is set on the block, the only concrete forming required is for the headwall construction, which sits on the block and goes around the bridge ends. Anchors for bridges over water can be easily tied into the headwall. The stability of the soil will also play a major factor in the construction of the bridge footings. A crane and large equipment are necessary for a project of this scale. Bridges that require extensive engineering to design will also require that a contractor build and install them. Small bridges can be built with park crews provided an engineer has reviewed the design and the crew has some talent for construction.

When estimating bridge costs, include the long-term maintenance costs for the life of the bridge. This will help to justify the purchase of the right bridge for a long life of low-maintenance service.

When a bridge is no longer cost efficient to repair or a new bridge is being designed, several questions should be asked:

1. Is the bridge necessary?

2. Who will use the bridge?

3. Does it need a handrail or guardrail?

4. If the bridge is going over a stream, is it small enough that stepping stones can be used in place of it or two large rocks with a small gap for the stream?

5. Can concrete, galvanized steel, or polyvinyl chloride (PVC) culverts take the place of a bridge? Culverts with high headwalls are just as good as a bridge, aesthetically and functionally, and they are a lot cheaper to maintain (see Fig. 6.6). Don't forget, concrete culvert pipe comes in some very large sizes in addition to the box, oval, and round styles.

6. If the bridge is the only alternative, are low-maintenance materials to be used?

Fig. 6.6

7. Can the bridge span be built without supports, which are maintenance concerns?

8. Is the soil and slope suitable for support if more than 10 or 15 feet of bridge span is required?

9. Can a prefabricated bridge be used or must it be built on site?

10. Consider what materials are needed for the bridge structure—pressure-treated lumber, laminated beam, steel, or concrete?

Consideration should be given to low-maintenance materials. All wood, for example, should be pressure treated and plastic lumber and metal should be hot-dipped galvanized to prevent rust stains on the wood and to reduce maintenance (see Fig. 6.7). Salt in snowy regions is a necessary evil that eats away at all exposed metal, such as beams or rebars embedded in concrete. In these situations, the metal should be accessible so it can be easily repaired and repainted if necessary. Generally, steel bridges are extremely rugged and almost maintenance-free. Wood is good for its natural appearance. Laminated wood, also called Glulam, is as strong as steel and is made of odd-length lumber joined with glue to create the desired length. Laminated wood is also lightweight and resistant to the harmful effects of salt. Glulam bridges are easy to install and have very low maintenance requirements. Cor-Ten is an alternative, low alloy steel that can also be considered for park use because it is quite resistant to corrosion, stronger than standard carbon steel, and has a very attractive, natural appearance. It requires minimal maintenance because any scratches will disappear as the metal ages.

2. **Management:** Bridge management must be periodic and regular. Someone must check all bolts, look for rust, repair all wood, check the decking and headwalls, look under the bridge, make all repairs, and perform all painting as necessary. Using pressure-treated 3 inch-by-8 inch decking planks for a footbridge will minimize deck replacements and last for 30 to 40 years, which is roughly the lifespan of a bridge. Bridges become focal points in parks (see Fig. 6.8), so every effort should be made to ensure a quality product is produced that is easy to maintain as well as beautiful to look at.

Bridge management can be a very expensive item in the park budget. The costs of maintaining vehicular bridges cannot be reduced without serious consequences. Maintenance and repairs to vehicular bridges are best left to professional engineers and contractors. Footbridges, on the other hand, offer considerable latitude for maintenance.

Fig. 6.7

Fig. 6.8

Retaining Wall Design

Whenever there is a steep grade covered with grass, a management problem exists. One of the alternatives for reducing management is to build a retaining wall. Sometimes a few small retaining walls are better than one large one, but this approach requires a lot more space and a level area between the top of one wall and the bottom of the next. Retaining walls can be "wet," using solid concrete or blocks, stones, timbers, metal plates, brick, and so on, or they can be built "dry," that is, constructed without mortar.

Regardless of the type of wall, a few basic rules on wall construction and safety must be followed. The wet wall should have a "batter" or slope of 1 inch into the embankment for every 1 foot of height. The dry wall requires 2 inches of batter for each foot of height. Batter is not necessary if the wall is less than 2 feet high. The wet wall requires a footing and solid material below grade and to the frost line. The footing should be one half to two thirds as wide as the wall is high. The dry wall will require only a 6-inch base of larger wall material and a layer of gravel below grade.

Both walls need a 4- to 6-inch drain pipe just below grade and behind the wall to prevent water from building up pressure and pushing the wall over. This drain must empty into the site's drainage system or at a dry well at the end of the wall. More elaborate and taller walls may require the placement of gravel or crushed rock behind the wall and around the drain pipe to pull off all excess water. The wet wall will also require weep holes going through the wall just above grade but any water behind the dry wall can seep through the cracks. Walls over 4 feet high will require a structural engineer to approve the design and will also require an anchor or deadman to ensure stability to the wall.

Dry walls are typically thought of as stone walls built by pioneering farmers as their earliest fences. The stone wall around the farmhouse was usually a double wall, and the herb garden was basically stone-free. This was because the farmer's wife usually picked out all the stones and dropped even the smallest ones into the space between the double walls. Because most of these stone walls have been in place for 200 years or more, they have become covered with moss and filled in with trees and are extremely picturesque. To look the same, new stone walls must be made of native stone and built in the same random pattern as the old walls were. The dry wall construction is much more difficult to build because the wall depends on weight, friction, and interlocking components to provide wall stability. When building a dry wall, of stone for example, start just below grade with the largest stone available. Be sure the row is in line. Each layer of rock can get smaller as the wall gets higher. Each stone must fit into the wall and be locked together with other stones and some soil. A stone or mortar capping can be put on the top of the wall to finish the top and keep out excessive moisture. Because clay soils hold so much water, they will exert more pressure on the wall than will sandy soils. Clay soils, therefore, cannot support as high a wall as those on sandy soils. As a final touch, mosses or rock garden plants should be planted in soil pockets between the rocks. Believe it or not, buttermilk can even be poured over the rock to encourage mosses to grow.

Mortared walls have to be built with the same standards and advantages or disadvantages as wet walls. Mortared walls can be made with materials such as bricks or stones that are mortared on all sides, and the resulting finished wall will be very formal in appearance. An alternative when using stones is to put them against a core of mortar in the middle of the wall. This will give the appearance of a dry stone wall but the strength of a wet wall. Another alternative to building walls against an embankment is to use concrete blocks and have stones or brick as an aesthetic face to the wall. With any type of mortared wall, a good footing is essential as well as a drainage system of weep holes, gravel, and drains.

There is also a whole category of precast wall that comes in a wide variety of colors, textures, shapes, stone lookalikes, brick lookalikes, and so on. Most of these precast units have notches, grooves, keys, or pins that hold the units together. Every manufacturer has its own patented design. These walls have the strength of a wet wall and the aesthetics and porous qualities of a dry wall. Some of these products will allow walls to be built 25 feet high. Regardless of the product selected, always follow the manufacturer's directions exactly.

Always check local building codes prior to constructing retaining walls. Many codes limit the wall's height. Many codes also require fencing or railings at the top of the wall. The codes will specify the depth of a wet wall to the frost line. Some codes will also limit the materials used on a wall.

Paver Design

Pavers of brick (see Fig. 6.9) or concrete blocks (see Fig. 6.10) project a sense of warmth, scale, and interest that is hard to equal with other materials. Brick and concrete's strength and durability are also important attributes. Visit the historic districts of many American cities and towns and you will see bricks that have been in place for a century or two and have withstood constant assault from traffic, weather, and other abuses. Bricks are usually baked clay, while pavers are made from cement. Occasionally, pavers can be stone blocks or made from asphalt. All pavers are similar in use and dimension and in this section the term is used to describe all varieties.

The installation of pavers is becoming increasingly popular as an alternative to concrete or asphalt for walkways, sitting areas, and public spaces. Interesting patterns can be created by mixing different colors to delineate spaces. Visual patterns can be created by using pavers of varying shapes or by installing pavers in one or more types of bond. The textural quality of a paved area is cre-

Fig. 6.9

Fig. 6.10

ated by varying the color and pattern. Pavers can also be used in combination with other types of pavement. For example, a concrete band alongside a brick walkway will accent both the color and the texture of the bricks, creating interest in the design.

Paver Installation

The manner in which pavers are installed contributes to the quality and success of the project. Pavers in public parks should be installed using the dry-laid method. This technique does not require years of experience. Figure 6.11 illustrates the brick walk installation steps while Fig. 6.12 shows the masons working in a large area. The key lies in the preparation of the base. First of all, excavation must extend to a depth that includes the thickness of the paver plus 3 inches. All topsoil must also be removed and replaced with compacted gravel. Remember to install PVC sleeves for existing utilities, irrigation, and future service within the subbase.

After the gravel is in place, the next step is to place a 3-inch layer of limestone screenings, crusher run, stone dust, or coarse sand. This layer must be well tamped, preferably with a vibrator. To get straight, even edges that do not undulate randomly, use forms of one-by-threes for straight runs and thin plywood for curves. Ryerson steel edging, plastic edging, and a wide range of similar products are available for use with bricks or pavers. Best results are obtained with edgings that are pinned into the base material. Their use can save considerable time and installation expense, but care must be taken to ensure that the edges are firmly secured. Minor variations in paver dimensions may require slight deviations from

Fig. 6.11

Fig. 6.12

the plan. Placing an edge brick on end (a sailor course) helps to ensure that the interior bricks will not migrate. The sailor course may be set in concrete for added stability. Even with edging, the sailor course should still be installed to present the appearance of a finished edge and a quality product.

After all the edges are set, it is time to prepare the final surface upon which the pavers will be laid. A "screed" is cut from a straight two-by-four and worked from side to side along the length of the forms to create an even, consistent grade on the base. Additional screedings may have to be added to low spots, which would then need to be rescreeded. Once the base is ready for pavers, it should be wet down to hold it in place.

Laying the pavers is the easiest part of the job. They should be laid hand tight, with joints that never exceed ⅜ inch wide. Each paver should be heavily tamped in with a rubber hammer or block of wood, with any adjustment for variation in paver height and width made at this time. Use a tight string to establish final grades, slope, and alignment. The string should also be used to ensure that each row of pavers remains straight and properly graded. Sand is then swept into the joints and washed in with a light watering. This process is repeated until the joints are completely filled. The only remaining tasks are to remove any temporary forms, backfill the edges, and sweep the surface clean.

Pavers that are set in mortar offer a more stable surface and one that may be easier to maintain, but their installation requires more time, effort, expertise, and expense. Excavation must be increased to accommodate a 4-inch concrete slab upon which the pavers will be laid. For drainage, a 6-inch gravel base is essential under the concrete. The concrete should be a mixed 1:2 cement/sand ratio. After the concrete hardens, a 1-inch setting bed of mortar is spread, with the pavers laid in the wet mortar. Joints are mortared as well, creating a solid, impermeable surface. The mortar should be a 1:3 cement/sand ratio. This method requires considerable masonry skill to produce a consistent surface with straight, even joints. A pitch of a least ⅛ inch per foot is necessary to avoid puddles during wet weather and ice problems in winter. Expansion joints must also be provided every 15 to 20 feet. Any broken pavers or separated joints that allow moisture penetration will be a point of eventual failure in the project.

References

"Pedestrian Bridges," *Grounds Maintenance,* July 1974: 26.

Phillips, Leonard E., "It's the Little Things That Count," *City Trees,* October 1985: 11.

"Retaining Traditions: New Looks for Walls," *Landscape and Irrigation,* February 1993: 22–25.

Stearns, Dan T., "Push for Pavers," *Landscape and Irrigation,* December 1993: 28–29.

PART 2
Management

7

Public Relations Programs

Public relations programs are necessary to keep park programs intact and to let the public know as much about the park department as possible. The following ideas will help preserve the public's perception of a department that is "on top."

An *open house* is an event that can show off the park department's equipment and its beautification programs. It can be held by one department or several city departments. The park department should have people available to discuss residential landscape maintenance concerns and address other problems. Pamphlets concerning local parks should be available for free distribution. Large photos of parks or park activities should be mounted on Velcro or thumb tack display boards to capture the public's attention. More specific information should then be available for those interested in learning more about what the photographs illustrate. Make the open house fun for the visitors.

Local parade officials usually call municipal departments to assist in setting up staging, closing streets, and related tasks. In addition to this service, why not spend one day of labor decorating a new flatbed park truck with a banner, shrubs, flowers, sod, and mulch on the bed or on a trailer and then enter it in the parade as a float? Tractors used in the parks can also be utilized to pull decorated trailers, as shown in Fig. 7.1.

Trucks and equipment should be kept clean, waxed, and repainted as necessary. Shiny equipment demonstrates the pride the department has in its operations and influences the public's perception of the department.

Uniforms for employees also reinforce this attitude of pride. They promote a clean, neat image for both the public and the employees themselves.

Fig. 7.1

"Life in a fish bowl" is an expression used to indicate that park departments are constantly in the public's eye. Be sure your employees do not all stand around while one person works. Keep the crews as small as possible and keep them working separately. Train the supervisors to observe the crews as a citizen might. Send employees to different coffee shops so hangouts don't develop. If trucks are brightly painted, consider less visible colors.

New projects should be encouraged. The willingness to take on additional responsibilities, with appropriate funding, creates a positive attitude in the public. It also emphasizes your labor skills and diversity. Employees like a change of pace, and it instills a healthy sense of higher importance over other municipal departments. However, it can also lead to a dependence by others on your department, which makes it difficult to cut your department at budget time.

Creative funding should be everyone's goal. Use parking meter receipts to pay for public parking lot landscaping. Garden clubs and civic organizations will often support special beautification projects. Sometimes these groups will assemble picnic tables or park benches. Encourage local neighborhoods and individuals to adopt a park to support and raise funds for their projects. Collect any vehicle accident damage to trees or public property from insurance companies. When doing work for other municipal departments find out if there are funds available to cover the park department's cost or at least obtain an IOU, payable at budget time. Submit bids to do the landscaping projects on municipal lands such as at the schools, housing projects, parks, highway projects, utility buildings, and so on. Make your department an important and vital link in the smooth workings of your city.

Planting funds should come from many sources. Use the greenhouse effect, summer drought losses, or any other current event to justify more money in your planting budget. Ask the garden clubs and other civic groups to help contribute to a tree planting fund or help plant flowers. Buy small containerized plants, and use the planting crew to teach volunteers from civic groups where and how to plant properly. Decrease the sizes of plants so more can be purchased. Increase the number of bare root plants being planted, provided the survival rate is kept high. Prune wild trees and shrubs into ornamental shapes or transplant them to the municipal nursery and park sites to eliminate the purchase price. Shop around before bidding to be sure there are plenty of plants in the variety and size you want. Common varieties are less expensive than scarce varieties. Plant more smaller plants in the parks where vandalism is less likely to be a problem. Have neighborhood kids help plant large trees in problem areas. The kids will develop a sense of "ownership" that will help protect the tree from vandalism attacks. Expand your supplier market by getting prices from nurseries 1000 or more miles away. The savings could more than pay the shipping costs provided the zone and climate matches yours. Purchase in quantity and wholesale. Combine your bid with other municipalities and your forestry department. Review bid specifications to look for cost savings and be sure the bids are prepared as unit items so quantities can be modified if the funding changes and so the awards can be given to those offering the lowest price for each plant.

Public displays such as display boards and slide shows should be sent to the library and city hall whenever special park projects or events warrant the attention or will draw a crowd. Permanent or long-term displays should also be considered.

Brochures should be prepared by the staff that discuss local concerns. They should look as professional as possible and be complete but to the point. Subjects should be timely and address current problems or explain new projects to your residents.

Local press and newspapers should be used for news releases that indicate who, what, where, when, and why. Press releases should be concise and provide the essential information. Include answers that explain who is doing something, what is being done, where it is going to be done and when, why it is being done, and finally who the contact person is, including their address and phone number. Local reporters should be called in advance so they can cover the event. A press release will give them the necessary facts. If something bad happens, the press should be greeted with prepared comments instead of "no comment," which suggests guilt.

Cable TV should be used as much as the local newspaper. The information on the press release should be spoken rather than read aloud, and the reporter can have prepared questions. Try to take advantage of the small viewing audience to have your spokesperson practice talking in front of the camera. Then, if a major event occurs that brings in the network news, he or she will be prepared and relaxed with the reporters and the cameras.

Speakers should be available to give talks on popular environmental subjects. The speaker should be a municipal employee who is well versed in the subject and possesses speaking skills. This employee should speak at any local club, civic organization, group, meeting, or get-together where residents would appreciate environmental information. The speaker should attend and give talks at regional or national trade conferences where the park department's reputation could be greatly enhanced.

In some cities *newsletters* containing local government news are mailed to every resident. Each department should prepare an article for every issue. This medium is especially effective for timely subjects such as spray programs, seasonal diseases, special events, tree planting programs, giving gifts to the city for special projects, and so on.

Publish all ideas, articles, awards, and the like in professional journals. This enhances the reputation of the department nationwide. Sending copies to your city leaders won't hurt either.

Utility bill stuffers can be a useful means of distributing newsletters if the water, sewer, or electric departments allow you access to their bills. This approach provides a low cost way to reach every residential unit with timely information about park events or problems, pest attacks, and other items of current interest. Keep in mind that people often throw away stuffers without looking at them and that bills are usually considered negative.

Public opinion surveys should be conducted to determine the public's perception of the department. A survey of one tenth of 1 percent of the local population or 2000 calls is more than sufficient to determine the attitudes of the public and any major problems they may have with the department. The survey will also highlight the department's success or at least the public's perception of success. Repeated surveys will provide guidance for the future and a way of tracking how far you have come.

Enter competitions so you can have an award-winning department. The coverage of such events both by the sponsor as well as the local press is always very positive.

Logos present an image that increases the public's recognition of an organization as one that is "on top." Logos for specific parks such as the Osprey of Horseneck Reservation in Westport, Massachusetts (see Fig. 7.2) also provide a strong identity.

Billboards are used by some communities to promote park and recreation programs. However, many environmentalists feel such a marketing medium is contradictory since billboards tend to aesthetically "litter" the landscape.

Mascots are used by many communities to help promote park programs and to teach people, children especially, about conservation principles. An example would be Woodsy Owl, who supports litter cleanup and uses the slogan "Give a Hoot, Don't Pollute." Many cities have their own mascots and slogans that help to inspire pride in the community.

A park's *office secretaries* must have excellent telephone manners because they convey the first impressions of the park to the public. Secretaries should also be informed about work crew and staff activities, department policies, and long-term projects. They should be able to impart as much—correct—information as they can.

Inquiries from *residents* should receive special attention and a reply by phone, letter, or in person. Respond promptly, factually, and courteously. Keep note of your appearance, tone of voice, and choice of words, and be sure to listen carefully to the questions and concisely answer the caller's specific question only. When citizens

HORSENECK
STATE
RESERVATION

*DIVISION OF ACQUISITION
AND
CONSTRUCTION*

Fig. 7.2

become irate, give them 15 minutes to calm down before calling them back.

Plant flowers at every possible location, especially in heavily used parks. Flowers draw attention to routine maintenance efforts. Make sure the maintenance of these flowers represents the best care available whether it is performed by volunteers, contractors, donations, or city labor. Even if the maintenance has been going on for years, it will never be noticed until it stops or until the flowers are not cared for.

Theme parks can vary in size from a few acres to a common theme used throughout a city to a park as large as Disney World. Theme parks will enhance the city's reputation on a scale proportional to the size of the park. While a local park department can develop theme parks as large as Aberdeen, South Dakota's Wylie Park (described in Chap. 1), the efforts of other localities have centered on specific plants or arboretums. One city has a weekend-long lilac festival that includes tours and vendors, while another is developing a theme park involving a popular plant that will be grown in every public space throughout the city. Tours are available that focus on one arboretum-park that has been developed over the years through donations, memorials, and gifts from residents, garden clubs, and other civic organizations. Other groups like to celebrate the city when a common plant is in bloom. Other variations of the theme park idea include window box competitions, traffic island beautification contests, and similar events.

Traffic islands usually consist of mowed grass or pavement. However, as described in Chap. 4, they can be converted to low-maintenance trees, shrubs, or flowers. This not only improves the environment but also encourages citizen praise for good work. Grass requires weekly mowing while heavily mulched shrubs, ground covers, or low-maintenance perennials can be visited once a month for a quick weeding. Traffic islands are extremely visible to city residents, and any work performed on them will be noticed by a lot of people.

Citizen activists are valuable allies whose support should be sought when proposing park improvements and maintenance projects to taxpayers and city officials. Such activists are especially useful for promoting and pushing support for the park department budget at city hall and for conducting special programs that require volunteers. Volunteers will be discussed in more detail in Chap. 9.

Public relations ideas also come from listening to the park department's staff and from professional organizations, seminars, and professional journals. This author, for example, gets most of his new ideas by attending an annual meeting-trade show closely related to his profession and by being active in that organization.

References

Forgacs, Sandra, "Public Relations Programs," *City Trees*, November 1988: 9.

Phillips, Leonard E., "Public Relations Programs Continued," *City Trees*, November 1988: 10.

8

Vandalism Prevention

What Is Vandalism?

Simply defined, vandalism is the willful destruction of property. Although it has been a problem for centuries, the increased occurrence of recent years has become appalling. Vandalism is not only increasing in every community and city in the United States, it has become an epidemic in many countries throughout the world.

Although a complete eradication of vandalism can never be achieved in a democratic society, it has been determined that 90 percent of all vandalism can be attributed to attitude problems that are preventable. The remaining 10 percent is malicious and therefore not easily controlled except by vandal-proof designs.

Historical Origins

The modern usage of the term *vandalism* is derived from the looting and plundering of a medieval tribe called the Vandals, who migrated from river valley to river valley throughout much of Germany. As their population and strength grew, they entered France in 406 A.D. and Spain in 409. From 429 to 439, they conquered and devastated the Roman-held lands of Africa, and in 455, under their king Genseric they invaded Rome and the city was looted and plundered for 14 days. The Vandals left Rome in ruins, destroying temples and palaces, carrying away gold treasures, and taking hostages for slaves. With the death of Genseric in 476, the Vandal empire began to decline and was finally defeated by the Byzantine army in 533. However, the Vandals' sacking of Rome was a pivotal moment in history, and it was because of this single event that any willful destruction of property is named vandalism today.

Types of Vandalism

Before solutions to vandalism can be found, it must be defined in as much detail and in as many different ways as possible.

Social science has categorized vandalism into the following related patterns:

Theft vandalism is the damage resulting from stealing money or materials.

Competitive vandalism is the damage resulting from games created in order to destroy something.

Philosophical vandalism is the damage resulting from a conscious tactic to deliver an ideological message or to gain some other theoretical result.

Malicious vandalism is the vicious and senseless damage resulting from rage or frustration.

Another way of looking at vandalism focuses on its targets, such as public facilities or institutions like schools, libraries, parks, and playgrounds. Other targets are often trees, bridges, golf courses, railroad cars and tracks, vacant buildings, and owner-unknown parked cars. Vandals often attack already derelict structures, which give the appearance of being unowned or abandoned.

Another definition of vandalism centers on a description of the type of individual perpetrating the vandalism and therefore the vandal's target. Vandalism is generally found in areas of low socioeconomic development, where the residents occupy a low-income occupational level and live in conditions of general instability, low morale, transience, and overcrowding. Vandalism often occurs where there is joblessness or boredom and where lives have no meaning or direction.

Vandalism is almost always caused by boys between 9 and 15 years old and between the hours of 4 P.M. and midnight. These young vandals seek status in an area where they can excel by retaliating against the establishment that they feel is against them. This misbehavior is also a symbol of masculinity in the eyes of the vandal as well as the eyes of his peers. Unfortunately, his environment provides few beneficial avenues for masculine achievement. Vandalism is to him only a mild form of violence and a means to achieve his masculine identity or gain acceptance into a gang, where his identity is reinforced. Middle- and upper-class vandalism appears to be a direct result of the male child lacking a positive masculine image. This is due to the father's preoccupation with his job or the long hours required to support the family. As with the working-class boy, the middle- or upper-class boy is also seeking a way to identify his masculinity. Again, the path to masculinity is found in vandalism.

The solution to vandalism, therefore, is complex and must address all facets of the vandal's life—his family, his peers, his school, his community, his free time, but most of all himself. In the school environment, vandalism occurs when students are frustrated and alienated and where there are no relationships or communication between students, teachers, administrators, and parents. Boredom, lack of interest in school, and peer pressure are added to the other pressures that are released in the form of vandalism. Boredom alone, recent studies indicate, is the cause of 80 percent of all vandalism. To oversimplify, in most cases vandalism is caused by frustrated boys striking out against a depersonalized object or the establishment they feel is responsible for their own lack of masculinity.

Common Solutions

The most common solutions to vandalism are not always the most successful and are aimed at preventing the act of vandalism rather than preventing youths from becoming vandals.

Some of the most common vandalism prevention techniques consist of the following:

1. A fortress design consisting of windowless concrete and steel construction is typically found in vandalism-prone neighborhoods. In terms of landscape protection, fortress design occurs in the form of fences, boulders, railroad ties, curbs, and concrete or steel bollards.

2. Clearing away the slums where vandals reside is another technique but one that fails to solve the problem because vandalism is a personal problem requiring a personal solution. The depersonalized "vandal-proof" facility needs to be humanized to be effective. This entails having people use the facilities. Governments need to show the public that buildings belong to all of the community's residents, and when vandalism does occur, buildings should be kept in good repair and the damage corrected immediately.

3. Another technique, lighting, can work in two ways. If lights are used, they should have grates or mesh covers and break-resistant lenses. The entire area should be heavily illuminated, including every potential hiding spot. On the other hand, some parks are better off in total darkness: any flashlights can therefore be identified as belonging to trespassers and vandals will be deprived of the light they do their work by. Moreover, totally dark sites have low energy costs. Motion detector lights are an option to consider if it can be ascertained that they will scare away potential vandals rather than provide them with the light they need to do their work.

4. Incident reports are useful for documenting vandalism attacks. Copies should be sent to local police departments and insurance companies if appropriate. Such reports should obviously be used to report damage but also to describe what techniques can be used to prevent a recurrence and to provide an action plan for repairs.

5. Developing increased security such as alarms, security systems or guards, fences with locked gates, attack dogs, and ready access throughout the facility for security patrols and emergency vehicles can also be effective. Dumpsters, sheds, fences, and other unnoticed items around a larger building are often used as a way of climbing onto the building roof and should be relocated. Every property owner should make a careful inspection of the facility for access prevention.

6. Publicity campaigns that highlight the costs of vandalism usually do not work! Separate courts that hear vandalism cases alone and release the names of vandals to the local press are only marginally more successful. Consider again the definition of who the vandal is. The publicity only draws attention to his act of vandalism, providing him with the recognition of his masculinity he has been seeking. Furthermore, advertising acts of vandalism at a specific facility only encourages repetition and increased vandalism and leads to an outraged public that becomes frustrated with the ever increasing problem of added damage and costs to repair public property and the potential for declining real estate values. On top of all this, techniques to suppress vandalism do not make it disappear: it only resurfaces in another location.

   The only positive impact of a publicity campaign is on the 1 percent of those families who get tough, who care, and who either try to reach out to help troubled youth or take a good look at their own children to be sure they know where their kids will be on Saturday night. Legal immunity to libel action in some states has resulted in police providing newspapers with the names of convicted vandals and their parents. This form of publicity has been somewhat successful in deterring second offenders because it makes the parents realize their problem and give their child the necessary help and attention.

7. Vandalism to landscape materials is often prevented by the use of fewer but larger trees, thorny plant material, and trees that readily resprout when damaged. Staking newly planted trees with steel posts or using cables on deadman will often prevent loss or damage. However, making nine-year-old boys plant the tree will promote pride and "ownership" that will ensure 24-hour protection for that tree until the boy and tree are both full grown.

   One rather unique solution to the theft of shrubs involves chaining them together. In one community, used chain from swing sets is laid down around newly planted shrubs. "S" hooks are used to connect a small loop around the shrub stem, and each end of the chain is hooked to a larger tree, a rock, or a post. The shrubs are all hooked together, and the chains are then covered with mulch. This solution will work all the time, and the worst that can happen is that one or two shrubs are pulled out of the ground in theft attempts, but the plants are not taken, and the entire bed is saved.

8. A rather unique vandalism prevention program was developed in the school department of Elk Grove, California. It provides a mobile home at certain schools for a "school sitter." In exchange for free rent, the mobile home resident patrols the school grounds after hours, and any suspicious activities can be quickly reported to the police. When this program was developed over 20 years ago, vandalism cost the Elk Grove school district $22,000 a year. Five years later, the vandalism bill for the year was $7500. Inflation has caused the amount to increase since then but not enough to consider dropping the program. The school-sitting idea has been spreading across the nation as a successful technique for curbing crime against school buildings.

It must still be emphasized, however, that none of these programs successfully helps the individual who becomes a vandal. They only reduce the damage after the child has established a record of vandalism.

Design Solutions

Design solutions address the act of vandalism rather than helping the troubled youth. However, due to the extent and complexity of design, and until the vandalism problem can be properly solved, prevention by design must be provided whenever new construction is considered. Nothing is vandal-proof. There are only vandal-resistant products, materials, equipment, and facilities. With this in mind, vandalism prevention and security should be considered for all new projects or for extensive remodeling projects. Even where vandalism is not a problem or has been significantly reduced by other programs, the life expectancy of a building could long surpass any vandalism prevention program.

Design solutions begin with an identification of the most commonly vandalized targets. Research by Dr. Monty Christiansen at Pennsylvania State University resulted in a list of vandalism targets in park and recreation facilities:

Restrooms	Shelters	Picnic tables
Waste containers	Benches	Walls
Drinking fountains	Lights	Electrical outlets
Fencing	Signs	Bleachers
Flagpoles	Guard railings	Sports and play apparatus
Bike racks	Plantings	

Once the vandalism targets have been determined, the selection of materials becomes the next concern. For example, wood is difficult to write on; gates and locks should only be used where curiosity may destroy what's behind the gate and lock; and concrete, brick, and steel are durable enough to withstand severe punishment.

In many communities, efforts to curb vandalism are continuous. After something is vandalized, it is replaced as soon as possible and in a manner that prevents recurrence. For example, in one city, the lifeguard tower at a local beach used to be a constant target for vandalism. This was resolved (see Fig. 8.1) with the construction of a concrete tower fabricated from some 5-foot-diameter precast manhole sections, stacked end on end to a height of 18 feet. Doors at the bottom and top permit entry, and the lifeguards can climb to the top using the interior manhole steps. While this solution might not look the best, it certainly eliminated vandalism to the tower.

Consideration should also be given to soliciting neighborhood input when considering the building of new facilities. Ask kids what they want and what it will take to get them to use a facility and use it right. Then do it. Other considerations for existing uses of a facility or property involve the following questions:

Fig. 8.1

Will the proposed project destroy the existing use, thereby subjecting the new facility to vandalism?

Is the proposed project such that no one would use it, again subjecting it to the threat of vandalism?

Consider alternative uses or abuses a facility will experience once the user has become bored with the proper use. After all, kids will not destroy what they want, like, and use. Also consider financial incentives: for every dollar *not* spent on vandalism repairs the same money can be spent on park improvements.

Vandals love to rip off roof shingles. One good solution to this problem is to make the roof inaccessible. Sometimes fences prevent access, but sometimes they are used to gain access. Another excellent prevention technique is the use of rolled roofing and heavily tarred joints sealed with nails every couple of inches, which prevent vandals' fingers from ripping out the shingles. Figure 8.2 shows a roof being replaced with rolled roofing.

Two techniques for keeping padlocks in parks or other places where they are wanted were successfully tried by the communities of Chicago and Wellesley, Massachusetts. The Chicago Park District turned to Master Lock's Rio Series to prevent break-ins. This lock has multiple keys and chambers that will fit into a very sturdy lock, and the lock and shank are extremely durable. The locks are coded so each park has its own series. Wellesley, Massachusetts, developed a program using the Best Lock. All the locks are purchased with long shanks. A malleable clamp is installed on the shank, and an 18-inch long piece of cable is attached to the shank with the same clamp. The other end of the cable is then attached to the fence or gate post where the lock is installed. A second malleable clamp is used to attach this end of the cable permanently to the fence or post. This procedure prevents the open lock from being thrown away, misplaced, used elsewhere, or otherwise vandalized. In the years since this technique was introduced, not a single lock has disappeared.

Maintenance and Use Solutions

Another solution to vandalism involves maintenance. Vandalism must be repaired as promptly as possible to present the appearance of pride in and care of the facility. A lack of maintenance suggests that no one cares, and this encourages addi-

Fig. 8.2

tional vandalism. Try to keep a facility open 24 hours a day. Even though most users would probably not report a vandalous act while it was occurring, people still provide the best deterrent to vandalism. The vandal cannot take the chance that other people will see him, recognize him, or report him. For the same reason, a facility should be visible from the surrounding neighborhood so residents can see and report acts of vandalism as they occur.

Landscaping provides an effective solution for hiding vandalism targets, for screening, and for controlling foot traffic. For example, plants can be used next to a building to eliminate hiding places, or low branches that vandals could hide behind can be raised, exposing the vandal's legs to the view of the facility's users. Thorns on plants are especially useful for discouraging hiding, blocking shortcuts, preventing trespassers from entering the property, and controlling unwanted foot traffic. Some excellent thorny plants include barberry, Oregon grape, juniper black locust and honey locust, hawthorn, holly, quince, firethorn, roses, devil's-walking-stick (aralia), Osage-orange, pear species, Jerusalem-thorn, and others. Use ivy or vines to cover the walls of vandalism targets: the vines make it difficult to spray paint or read vandalized walls. For unknown reasons, vandals seldom attack brightly colored objects. Painted picnic tables experience half the number of problems as those with natural wood colors. Brilliant walls of greens, blues, and reds have fewer vandalism problems than do brick, concrete, or wooden walls.

An understanding of why vandalism occurred in one city led to a solution of this problem. Kids wanted to have beach parties on spring evenings, and, with the beach locked, they broke down the gate and everything else. To solve the problem, a city employee was assigned to a 4 P.M.-to-midnight shift from April 15 until the beach opening date. The assignment allowed the employee to continue work begun during the day shift and also provided an unofficial watchman to prevent the annual vandalism problem. With someone there, the kids can now get into the beach and have their parties—if they control themselves and cleanup afterward. If problems occur or the party continues after midnight, the employee has radio access to the police.

Another problem was solved by determining the cause of vandalism at a city's high school athletic fields. Every Monday morning during the fall months, either the soccer goals or the football goals were wrecked. After talking to the teams, city officials discovered that there was a rivalry between the soccer and football teams: when the soccer team lost a Saturday game, it knocked down the football goals and vice versa. The coaches were notified, and the vandalism was immediately eliminated. Communication was a key to the solution.

Unfortunately, many agencies, municipal departments, school districts, and other vandalism victims can only provide common solutions—design solutions at best—to deter vandalism of their own facilities. The big solution has to be accomplished "by others" because it is not "in their jurisdiction." Although this excuse might be true insofar as a proper solution has to cut across everyone's jurisdiction, if a total program is to work each department has to do its share until the necessity of establishing a total community program hits home.

Successful Solutions

The successful solutions discussed in this section illustrate attempts to reach the youths responsible for causing vandalism before a problem occurs.

Crime watch programs encourage youths to observe and report acts of vandalism. Having community's youth participate in beautification projects and improvement programs encourages pride and a sense of ownership. Park directors also need to understand how drugs and gangs work. What are their motivations? What are their current levels of activity and strength? Who are the drug dealers and gang leaders? What drugs are being used? What local work is being done to solve these concerns, and how can the park's resources help? Restitution programs require the convicted vandal to repay, rebuild, or repair his damage. This solution comes the closest to reaching the root of the problem. Unfortunately, by this time it is too late to prevent the vandalism.

Another action that governments and employers can take involves hiring from the local labor pool. Not only does this promote feelings of good will, and hence lower vandalism rates, it also reduces local unemployment and promotes support from the local community. Local laborers know about local problems, local gangs, and local drug activity. They can direct the employer in a way that will help the community and prevent harm to the employer's facilities. Local labor will also take pride in maintaining local employment.

Another very successful approach involves planting trees. Tree planting is a very nonthreatening event that can reduce conflicts between groups and improve community relations. Planting trees develops a sense of pride and involvement. Trees planted by local residents are appreciated and protected for the benefit of all. Planting programs also develop a sense of community because as people work together they solve problems together and take care of each other. Tree planting programs sometimes encourage residents to become involved in crime watch campaigns, recycling efforts, youth programs, and other efforts to improve the environment of our cities.

Baltimore County, Maryland, is one example of a community with an active environmental improvement program that includes tree planting. Trees are planted along city streets as well as on county-owned and abandoned properties. All the planting efforts are coordinated with cleanup efforts, and minority residents participate in the tree-planting program. The program develops high levels of pride as well as improving the city environment.

One solution to vandalism is the prosecution of convicted vandals. Most vandals are never caught, and of those that are, most are never convicted. Why? Because the crime is committed without witnesses, because the object of the act of vandalism is property and not a person, and because the offender is usually a young boy—a juvenile according to the law, which tends to be lenient with juveniles. Because of such laws, kids know that even if caught they will only be remanded to the custody of their parents, who probably don't care anyway.

With this in mind, consider a successful solution. Every community must have a communitywide vandalism prevention program in which every boy aged 9 to 15—those statistically most likely to become vandals—is encouraged to participate. The program could include requiring the boy to join a scouting group, school or church organization, band, sports program, or community service or civic organization. Any form of character-building organization, job, or social center should be available so these boys can have friends and search for their identity in constructive ways—organizations where they can enhance their personal pride and their sense of accomplishment, develop a sense of community pride, and find their masculinity.

In one community, government leaders cooperate to sponsor a work center where young boys not belonging to any other organization get involved in projects that improve the community's facilities. These projects include painting and constructing park and recreation facilities, repairing school facilities, and any number of other projects easily arranged by the work center's leaders. Dull or repetitive projects are avoided because they result in dissatisfaction and, therefore, a worse attitude among the boys than they had before. Participants in the program are also used as valuable assets in the design of new or remodeled facilities, for not only can they provide necessary insight into potential vandalism targets, they can also be used to solicit potential users' comments as well as project support. Having a voice in the project's design or participation in its construction promotes a sense of pride and responsibility in the successful development of the project. Youths who feel that a part of themselves has been involved in a project will defend it to the end. Vandalism caused by poor attitude can be prevented by improving the youth's personal attitude as well as his pride in the community. One of the best ways to accomplish this is to get youths as well as adults involved in volunteer projects that pertain to community facilities and programs. These projects should enhance the individual's civic pride as well as his pride in accomplishment and should be geared not only toward the individual volunteer but to groups of volunteers such as school classes, Boy Scouts, and community service organizations with a youth membership.

Some typical projects might include the following: tree planting; flower box competitions; picnic table and sidewalk bench construction; spring cleanup projects for streets, parks, and government buildings; painting projects; tree and brush clearing; programs for adopting a park or traffic island for year-round care; recreation program leadership; street sign inventory and replacement; trail development or maintenance projects in parks; programs providing assistance to city agencies or consultants requiring municipal studies or public opinion surveys; and weeklong, in-depth tours of the local government.

The list is endless, as any city administrator will admit. However, only those projects that will promote pride of accomplishment and pride in the community should be selected. If the volunteer is given a dull or repetitive project, he might leave it half-finished and with less pride and a worse attitude than before he started.

Objections to using volunteers in vandal prevention programs are likely to come from local labor unions, who see volunteers taking work away from their membership. However, such problems can be avoided by conducting the program as a government-sponsored vandalism prevention program for troubled youth rather than a make-work program to provide free labor. This problem can also be avoided by clearly indicating to the unions which public projects are for union members and which are for the youth program. The unions should be encouraged to support the program in the beginning, especially if they can be made to see the volunteers as potential union members if they later join the workforce. Unions can also be encouraged to support community service programs, thus softening their opposition (unless they see the programs as a contract violation).

Other successful projects that primarily address the youths themselves and view the acts of vandalism as a secondary issue have been implemented in several communities around the country. Some of the best are described in the following paragraphs.

Burlington, Massachusetts, participates in a program called National Youth Program Using Minibikes. This delinquency prevention program was begun in 1969 and has proved its value in over 400 communities nationwide. The program provides a recreation outlet for troubled youngsters between 11 and 15 years of age. Participants must sign a contract for good behavior in exchange for the privilege of using a donated minibike for two hours a week. Those who fail on their contract are punished by becoming "outcast" spectators instead of "in-group" participants.

Adventure playgrounds have been popular in Europe in recent years and have provided opportunities for releasing the constructive and destructive urges of children. It has been documented that these playground facilities have substantially reduced vandalism over the long run in their neighborhoods. In this country, adventure playgrounds have not been successful largely due to their aesthetics. With kids building and tearing down forts, houses, and whatever else their imaginations desire, such playgrounds do look bad. However, one site in Europe is enclosed with a high brick fence that has succeeded in preserving as well as hiding the playground. This may solve the aesthetic problem in this country.

Baltimore school students learn about laws, crime, and law enforcement in the city's Friendly Officer Program. The students meet police officers and during the course of the program improve their attitudes toward the police. Some students actually look into possible careers in law enforcement. This program and those very similar to it are very popular throughout the United States.

Aggression against the impersonality of educational, governmental, or institutional facilities can be successfully prevented by permitting access to these facilities to the neighborhood, to minorities, and to the economically deprived. Access to facilities for athletic or cultural pursuits can help to change the educational, governmental, or institutional image from that of an impersonal facility to a property "belonging to the neighborhood." Even something as simple as weekly tours of these facilities helps to promote neighborhood understanding and acceptance. Many schools have also found success by opening their gymnasiums to basketball games for local kids.

Roulston & Company, Inc., a Cleveland, Ohio-based investment company, best illustrated this principle when it moved its operation into a warehouse in a run-down, high-crime neighborhood. To prevent problems and ensure acceptance by the neighborhood, the company's executives went door to door throughout the neighborhood chatting and explaining who the company was and what they were planning to do. The program worked so well that the site has experienced virtually no vandalism, and its neighbors continue to protect the building.

Conclusion

The successful vandalism prevention program should consist of the following steps:

1. A meeting of all interested community leaders should be held to develop a program and request support for the implementation and continuation of a vandalism prevention program.

2. A youth program director or vandalism prevention program coordinator should be selected who can keep track of all boys who are statistically likely to become vandals and who can tailor the program to the local community.

3. The coordinator should follow through by constantly checking that the boys are matched to an activity or a character-building organization that provides them with a means of establishing their identity and masculinity.

4. The program should be run initially for a three-year trial period and continue indefinitely unless statistics indicate that the program is not cost effective in terms of preventing damage that might have occurred or is occurring in neighboring communities.

5. The coordinator should also coordinate the efforts and manage the cross jurisdictional concerns of the many community service, municipal, and other interested organizations to find projects and solve common problems.

Hopefully, these ideas will inspire municipal departments, churches, organizations, companies, and individuals to be aware of the statistical likelihood of vandalism and join in common action to prevent vandalism before it occurs. Gangs and drug abuse are problems that are a reflection on our society, our families, and our communities. The solution is not simple but requires supreme efforts from everyone—churches, civic organizations, schools, families, youth services, social programs, and many others at all levels of American society.

Graffiti

Vandalism that results in graffiti presents special problems. Since the introduction of aerosol spray paint, graffiti removal has become extremely difficult. Much of the spray paint, especially if it is fresh, can be removed with mild detergent, muriatic acid on masonry surfaces, or petrochemicals such as gasoline or mineral spirits. However, if the paint has hardened or if the surface is porous, removal is much more difficult. If powerful cleaning agents or solvents do not remove the paint, then sandblasting, rotary wire brushes, or the repainting of the entire surface becomes necessary—very costly solutions for a 5-minute act of vandalism.

Chemical Removers

There are several chemical products on the market that work reasonably well to remove graffiti. These products remove ink, crayons, lipstick, pencil, marker, tape marks, road tar, waxes, spray paint, and scuff marks from walls, walks, road signs, washrooms, counters and desk tops, vehicles, mirrors, lockers, concrete structures, and all metal surfaces. Although they work only on the surface, they are effective on most graffiti targets. They are not recommended for plastic, asphalt, or unfinished wood surfaces because they will remove any original dye, ink, or paint that should be there and they can also stain any colorless surfaces.

The application of these products involves spraying the liquid or aerosol on the graffiti or applying it to a cloth and rubbing it on the mark. If the surface is porous, it must be scrubbed with a stiff bristle brush before being wiped dry. Difficult marks may require a second application or a longer rubbing time. Such products contain acetone, butoxyethanol, toluene, or 1,1,1–trichloro-ethane, so they should always be used in a clean, well-ventilated area.

Paint strippers are an optional chemical remover that work fairly well. These products are formulated to remove all types of paint from most masonry, stone, metal, and wood surfaces. They penetrate the paint and can be flushed away with a high-pressure water blast after a short period of time. They should not be allowed to dry on the surface. Paint strippers contain methylene chloride and methanol.

One word of caution should be heeded when using these products. The vapors from some products are harmful, and the liquid is fatal if swallowed. It is also a good idea to test the chemical in an isolated location first to be sure it will not harm the surface. Be sure the container and cloths are discarded according to applicable statutes. All chemical removal products should be used in well-ventilated areas. Rainsuits, gloves, boots, and face shields are recommended to prevent the chemical's contacting the eyes, skin, and mucous membranes.

Environmentally Safe Removers

Environmentally safe removers contain no EPA-listed hazardous materials and are nontoxic, biodegradable, nonflammable, water soluble, and have a low odor level. They are especially useful on painted, hard finish surfaces but are not recommended for use where water-based latex paint has been applied. They are especially good on brick and masonry surfaces. New graffiti can be emulsified in as quickly as 20 seconds; old paint may take 5 minutes. These products do not evaporate quickly. They are made with natural terpene and are available in liquid or gels. Care must be taken on some plastic surfaces to be sure these products do not soften or emulsify the undercoat. They will remove latex, alkyds, vinyls, polyurethanes, and once the products set they can be removed with cloths or high-pressure water.

Environmentally safe removers should be used with care, soiled cloths should be disposed of, and workers should always work toward the center of the graffiti area to avoid spreading the cleaners on nonvandalized surfaces. Prolonged exposure to these products should be avoided, as should contact with the skin and eyes. Goggles and nitrite rubber gloves should be worn when working with these products. Most can also be used as engine degreasers and gum and glue removers.

Water Cleaning

Water cleaning graffiti-removal techniques work by directing a blast of water ranging between 5000 and 36,000 psi at the graffiti. Most graffiti is removed at around 10,000 psi using about 5 to 6 gallons of water per minute. The water blast cuts right through most graffiti, rinses it away, and leaves a smooth, clean surface. Some systems work with steam or hot water, but most are cold water washers. The beauty of this method is that there are no chemicals, solvents, toxins, safety systems, or disposal procedures involved. This system can therefore save considerable amounts of money, especially in areas where graffiti is a major problem.

The heart of a water-blasting system is a high-pressure pump, powered electrically or with a diesel engine. The lances, nozzles, high-pressure hose, and valve systems must be of high quality to ensure the safety and longevity of the equipment. The major disadvantage of this approach is the cost and size of the equipment.

Wet Sandblasting

Because dry sandblasting has been banned by the EPA due to dust inhalation problems, a new technology involving water mixed with sand has emerged. Wet sandblasting uses the same silica sand as the dry method. The blasting machine operates at 3000 psi with flows of water up to 10 gallons per minute and uses a slurry of water and abrasive. The slurry is pumped through a jetting head gun. Using the wet method, the sand and paint fall to the ground directly under the surface being cleaned. This provides an easy and safe cleanup, and the sand can easily be cleaned up and reused. Because operators work with dust-free products, breathing apparatuses are not required. Safety glasses and protective clothing, however, are necessary for operator safety.

Other systems require that the sand be absolutely dry, with the water added at a mixing head. Such systems cannot recycle the abrasive material. Round sand particles of silica are the best for removing graffiti, and the size of the particles should be between a #20 and #40 screen mesh. During the removal process the jetting head gun should be aimed straight on the surface or at an angle of no more than 30° from straight on.

Clear Coating

Another graffiti-removal technique is to coat graffiti targets with a clear, nonglossy protective coating. This coating prevents paint, marker, and other materials from penetrating the surface. If graffiti occurs, this water-based, nontoxic coating can be easily removed and a new coating can be reapplied on the unharmed surface.

Prevention

Prevention is the best way to deal with graffiti. The solution to the graffiti problem begins with the question, who perpetrates graffiti and what is the target? Landscaping offers an effective design solution to hiding graffiti targets: thorns can control access to targets and planting vines or ivy against the wall of a graffiti target is an especially useful technique. Surveys have shown that the use of "graffiti boards" or allowing the painting of New York City subway trains has not had any appreciable effect on the amount of graffiti found elsewhere in the community. As a result, the legal spray painting of New York trains has been disallowed.

References

Christiansen, Dr. Monty, "Vandalism," *Park Maintenance*, September 1979: 10–11.

Greenbaum, Stuart, "Safe Park Principles and Practices," *Parks and Recreation*, March 1991: 49–52.

Kidby, Phillip, "Vandal Resistance Should be an Important Goal," *Parks and Grounds Management*, January 1994: 18–21.

Sarkisian, Sevan, "Coping with Park Vandalism," *American City & County*, August 1982: 49–50.

Yarmon, Morton, "Ideas that Can Cut School Crime," *Parade*, December 9, 1979: 11–15.

9

Volunteer Programs

Although most communities have full-time park staff capable of maintaining open space, other activities that require large amounts of time, effort, and labor make demands that are often beyond the capabilities of park staff. Getting these projects implemented while paid staff can concentrate on more pressing demands can be accomplished by using volunteers. Volunteers are people. They are usually good, conscientious workers looking for an educational, social, enjoyable, and gratifying experience. Volunteers want to feel appreciated and should feel as though they are making a contribution to their community.

Pros and Cons of Volunteers

The major disadvantage of using volunteers is the inability and unwillingness of some cities to insure volunteers against injury. Most states have settled this issue by stipulating that anyone who does work for another is covered by that employer's worker's compensation plan. However, because many cities are self-insured, they have chosen not to include volunteers as employees, even though volunteer supervision would prevent any claim of gross negligence.

Experience has proved, however, that volunteers actually have better safety records than paid employees. The reasons for this are threefold:

1. Volunteers work without time limitations and pressure to get the job done, so while the work may take longer, there is less carelessness and fewer shortcuts, which can cause accidents.

2. Volunteers are seldom given the opportunity to use heavy or dangerous equipment.

3. Volunteers are volunteering because they want to participate in a municipal project without costing taxpayers like themselves additional tax burdens. Using this same philosophy, volunteers who get injured will usually go to their own physician rather than file a claim against the city that, in turn, might burden the taxpayer. Using the worker's compensation issue as a reason not to use volunteers is therefore invalid.

Labor unions, however, have traditionally been opposed to the use of volunteers because they see them taking work and overtime away from dues-paying members. Successful volunteer programs have been able to avoid such union problems by adopting one or both of the following methods:

1. Before establishing a volunteer program, city officials meet with union officials to get their endorsement of the program. Once the union has approved, with or without conditions and limitations, the program can grow rapidly and without opposition.

2. Volunteers can be used to perform projects formerly done by union labor. Most employees will recognize that the volunteers are supplementing their efforts and that without their help these special projects would not get done. However, this approach runs the risk of inciting union opposition, with or without cause, at any time and with a considerable amount of unfavorable publicity if the union chooses to make an issue of the program.

The Volunteer Program

In the early 1970s, President Nixon promoted a Volunteers In Parks or VIPs program. In the late 1970s, these VIPs were called Parkateers, and during his administration President Bush referred to volunteers as a "thousand points of light." Regardless of the name, when properly utilized volunteers can be a valuable resource.

A successful volunteer program requires the development of a plan that uses volunteers to their best advantage as well as a central program coordinator who will encourage more volunteers to participate. The coordinator should organize the program and then provide training, recognition, supervision, and evaluation of the volunteers. Volunteer programs will not reduce a park's budget unless the volunteers displace paid staff. Volunteers offer the potential to make more productive use of existing funds and personnel because they enable the staff to increase the level and quality of all services delivered.

Seeking volunteers is not the first step in a volunteer program. The first priority is the establishment of a set of goals and objectives, such as developing a park master plan. Next, the time and task requirements of the program should be determined. Goals that are three years away might be unrealistic and discouraging to the volunteer, but goals six months apart provide a desirable incentive. Keep in mind that while there are many advantages to using volunteers, a major disadvantage will be the very slow rate of progress. The volunteer program should therefore be organized to respond to the motivations of volunteers and linked to the structure of the agency. Management of a volunteer program is a job in itself, which requires time, planning, education, and training.

The components of a good volunteer program are the following: record keeping, formulation of job descriptions, recruitment, interviewing, placement, orientation, training, supervision, dealing with staff, motivation, recognition, retention, and evaluation. These are described in more detail in the following sections.

Record Keeping

A system must be set up to organize the records of the entire volunteer program. The records should keep track of the volunteers, the jobs, the retention efforts, and the service and training records of the volunteers. Such records are also necessary to document legal responsibilities, accountability, and evaluations. Volunteers' records should be considered confidential.

Job Description

Volunteers need a description of the tasks they are expected to perform. When working in parks, for example, volunteers might be expected to perform weeding, mowing, flower care, pruning, trash cleanup, and the like for a particular park. However, the job description can also include items such as a job title, working hours or time requirements, goals, training, responsibilities, qualifications, benefits, and supervision. Job descriptions are also useful for publicizing volunteer activities while at the same time creating a clear distinction between the volunteer and paid staff job duties. The job description can also be used to define the monetary value of the volunteer labor. This value can be used to justify the entire volunteer program.

Recruitment

A recruitment program should attract potential volunteers from the entire community. Efforts to seek volunteers include radio and newspaper articles and advertisements, visits to the senior citizens office, municipal brochures and public service announcements, and word-of-mouth referrals. Many volunteers can come from court restitution programs. Other volunteers might come from the academic requirements for community service within certain courses or at certain schools. A catchy logo like the one illustrated in Fig. 9.1 will help recruit volunteers. Once a potential volunteer has come forward, an application form will be useful for defining the training, skills, and background of the volunteer. This information will be used to match the applicant with the job. Often the volunteers might have their own ideas about a specific area or function to include in the program. In such cases, the formal job description and placement efforts need to be modified. Recruitment efforts should also be directed toward obtaining volunteers with appropriate backgrounds for the jobs available. With the increasing demand for

Fig. 9.1

volunteers and the limited supply of potential volunteers, the recruitment process can become very challenging indeed.

Besides obtaining individuals for volunteer work, the program should also consider volunteer groups. These groups can come from civic organizations, church groups, school groups, parent/teacher organizations, garden clubs, scouts of all ages, businesses and contractors, landscape maintenance and tree care companies, and local nurseries and garden centers. When contacting these various groups, don't forget to accept donations in lieu of volunteers.

Interview

Once an applicant has applied, he or she should be interviewed. The most important question to ask applicants is why they want to volunteer. The answer to this question will give clues to the applicants' motivation and, hence, the proper form of recognition for their work. The interview will clarify the expectations of the volunteer while the municipality can use it to carefully screen and select volunteers. The interview will determine how the desires, skills, and capabilities of the volunteers relate to the needs of the municipality and the jobs available.

Placement

Volunteers need to be very carefully matched to the tasks available so as to satisfy the needs of the volunteer as well as the municipality. Follow-up and supervision are also required to ensure compatibility between the task and the volunteer. Careful planning is essential so the volunteer has a reasonable project, all the necessary tools, a time table, and the training required for success.

While no one likes a dull or repetitive project, the experienced volunteer or paid employee will know how to complete these assignments more successfully than new personnel. Projects should be assigned so the volunteer remains interested, enthusiastic, and proud of his or her work. Don't be afraid to confront the volunteer if things are not going smoothly. Often problems involve a simple misunderstanding or a bad assignment. If it is the latter, make a change.

Orientation

On the first day, volunteers should be given an orientation program to learn the duties and responsibilities expected of them. Because they often lack experience working in government, the orientation program will familiarize them with operations, procedures, and the other employees. Volunteers may not want to follow the "rules" and because social interaction is part of the fun of volunteering, managers have to respect this fact and encourage volunteers to work together. Paid staff should not be working too close together if productivity from volunteers is required. On the other hand, having volunteers work with paid staff is not a good idea either since paid staff will have higher productivity expectations than the volunteer is willing to provide or volunteers may be offended if the paid staff is not working hard enough.

Training

Training leads to a knowledgeable and skilled volunteer. The training program should consist of orientation followed by an overview of the municipal operations followed by a study of the details of the project area. In-service training will show the volunteers how to put theory into practice and will teach them the skills they will need to meet the requirements of the job description. If the training session is truly useful, it can bring staff and volunteers together.

Supervision and Communication

Clear lines of communication and supervision are essential in volunteer programs. Volunteers need to know who to communicate with so the paid staff is not offended and volunteers are not misdirected. Clear communication of supervisory roles clarifies the line of authority and facilitates accountability. Supervision of volunteers is best handled by a volunteer services director who communicates directly with paid staff through their chain of command. Because volunteers usually work different hours than paid staff, overlapping supervision is usually not a concern.

Motivation and Recognition

Volunteer recognition ceremonies and other incentives provide a modest form of appreciation. Some communities with effective volunteer programs find the most success with an inexpensive volunteers' picnic, at which the volunteers meet each other as well as the paid staff, and certificates can be awarded for volunteer achievements. Some major cities offer incentives for volunteers such as free gate admissions, free admission for guests, access to the employee cafeteria, parking privileges, uniforms, reimbursement for expenses, invitations to office parties, special classes, early admission to special events, and other incentives as varied as the communities themselves. Recognition incentives can also include a suggestion box; reimbursement for expenses; attention to personal needs and problems; recognition by the local press; taking time to talk; sending holiday cards; saying thank you; and the presentation of inexpensive awards such as certificates, flowers, bulbs or plants, photographs, and other small tokens of appreciation. Photographs of the volunteer at work sent to the local press reward the volunteer and encourage others to participate. Other events that can be considered for volunteers include seminars and walks or tours with nature or environmental themes. Above all, volunteers need to be given a positive image to identify with.

Evaluation and Retention

An evaluation of the volunteer program as a whole is as important as the evaluation of individual volunteers. Evaluations of individuals should focus on the attainment of the program's stated goals as well as the needs, growth, and satisfaction of the volunteer.

The evaluation of the volunteer program itself should begin with a survey of the volunteers that evaluates the training program, the usefulness of the program itself, and the pros and cons of the program and its specific assignments. The program should also be analyzed to determine its cost effectiveness through a comparison of the dollar value of donated labor versus the administrative and expense costs.

Evaluating employees is a difficult task for municipal employers because of the latter's reluctance to appear to question the well-meaning intentions of the volunteer's efforts. However, evaluations do guide the volunteers toward improving their pursuit of worthwhile and visible results. Allowing inappropriate behavior, mistakes, or mismatched assignments to continue without comment is an insult to the volunteer. A positive evaluation may promote volunteer renewals as well as an expansion of the volunteer program.

Tasks

There are a wide range of tasks that volunteers can perform to assist the staff of a park department. Volunteers can prune, water, and plant flowers, shrubs, and new trees and volunteer crews can be sent into overgrown parks to manage the trees through selected removals and careful pruning and thinning out of the brush. Volunteers are especially useful for celebrations or public relations campaigns that involve speaker lists and slide shows. They can give tours, do research, and perform other miscellaneous tasks as necessary. They can also be used for special projects where a large number of people are necessary to handle special events, such as potting plants for a spring sale or setting up special events in parks or recreation programs. Most park departments have enormous labor requirements and many projects suitable for volunteer adoption.

Modified Program

Smaller cities can develop volunteer programs to assist with very specific programs such as Adopt-a-Park or Adopt-a-Traffic-Island. By their nature, these programs can get by with a less sophisticated volunteer program than that outlined earlier in this chapter. Record keeping, placement, orientation, training, supervision, motivation, recognition, and retention, however, are important even in small programs with only one or two volunteers. Regardless of the size of the volunteer program, everything done by a volunteer is something that would otherwise not have been done or would have been done much later.

Citizen Activists

Many citizens are valuable allies who should be used to promote parks and open space management among other residents. Citizen activists are especially useful for promoting and planning support for the park budget at city hall and for conducting special programs that use volunteers. Park boards and advisory committees, for example, are usually comprised of volunteers.

Keep in mind that one enthusiastic volunteer can organize an entire committee just through word of mouth. A volunteer's pride will increase the group's desire to complete the initial assignment and then encourage others to volunteer as well. According to Margaret Mead, "We live in a society that always has depended on volunteers of different kinds—some who can give money, others who give skills, full time or part time. If you look closely, you will see that almost anything that really matters to us, anything that embodies our deepest commitment to the way human life should be lived and cared for, depends on some form—more often, many forms—of volunteerism."

Successful Volunteer Programs: Schenectady's Indian Meadows Park

In suburban Schenectady, New York, Indian Meadows Park was built and maintained entirely by volunteers. The project began when the town government appointed an 18-member board to select a site and coordinate its purchase with local, gift, state, and federal funds. The volunteers prepared a master plan and then went after gift funds to build access roads. They performed the actual site clearing and landscaping and convinced local baseball leagues to build ball fields and service clubs to build ice rinks, picnic tables, and shelters. Scouts and high school students in a nature education class built footbridges and developed nature trails. The local volunteer fire department and auxiliary cleared and seeded an area for hillside sledding. The local grange created a bird sanctuary with plants donated by the Soil Conservation District. Eventually, the town appropriated enough money to provide a groundskeeper to operate the donated lawn mower and provide other maintenance the volunteers could not do. The only drawback of the entire Indian Meadows project was the 10 years it took to accomplish at little taxpayer expense what could have been done in two years with a well-funded operation.

References

Mah-Kooyman, Shirley, "Volunteers, Establishment and Facilitation of a Valuable Resource," *City Trees*, January/February 1991: 18.

Mead, Margaret, "Do We Really Need Volunteers?" *Redbook*, September 1975: 60.

10

Growing Annuals and Perennials

For the park superintendent, the most important goal is that city residents recognize that a landscape is being maintained well. The planting of flowering plants is one way to accomplish this. Flowering plants provide many benefits to the landscape and the effective use of such flowers can set one city apart from others. Annuals, perennials, and ornamental grasses in particular provide color and year-round interest; can be changed periodically; come in a wide variety of sizes, colors, textures, and shapes; attract butterflies; have a pleasant fragrance; make excellent cut flowers; and are useful elements in landscape design. Above all, they promote pride in the city, pride in the park department, and pride in the groundskeepers taking care of them.

Design

The first step in creating a garden is arriving at the design. The design process begins with an examination of the planting site and its environmental conditions. Look at the soil. Is it wet or dry? Measure the shade and sun over a day. What about the topography and winds? Look at reflected light and heat from nearby walls. Are there trees nearby with roots that will compete with the plants? What colors, types of plants, and textures are right for the site? Is there a focal point in the garden or is one necessary? Is the garden bordered by a path that will draw your attention through or past the garden?

Make the design to scale so the number, variety, and locations can easily be determined. The size of the bed can also be determined so the amount of fertilizer needed can be calculated. Consider the design style. Is the park formal, informal, or naturalized? Formal parks are rigid and balanced. Designs for informal or naturalized parks should flow smoothly and there should be no sharp angles. Is the flower bed visible to the public? How will people see the display—will they walk or drive by the garden? The plants in informal beds should be grouped in odd numbers such as three, five, seven, or nine unless large beds are being prepared. Formal beds have equal numbers, sheared plants, and sharp edges. Keep in mind that the amount of available maintenance can affect the design styles. While historical trends have focused on the formal, the 1990s are following a less formal, lower maintenance garden style.

Ask yourself whether the design should involve the massing of a single species or a complicated design of many species. Mass plantings are useful for impact and drive-by viewing, while details hold attention and require benches and paths. Annuals and perennials also work well in combination with shrubs and woody plants. Plants with long blooming periods are especially useful in borders and masses as well as with shrubs. When selecting a plant, consider its foliage, color, texture, flower, and plant size. Also consider the features of the backgrounds and the scale or relationship between a plant and its background. Backgrounds are useful for screening bad views and emphasizing the positive elements in the garden. Color use in the 1970s and 1980s focused on bright hues, while the trend in the 1990s has been on soft tones and different tones and textures of green. The current movement toward using the popular ornamental grasses typifies this trend. Good design creates a balance of interest with variety, colors, and textures.

Annuals and perennials should be planted according to a design with a specific purpose. Is the planting intended to frame a view, highlight a building, be a focal point, enhance a sign, provide a border for shrubs or trees, or just brighten up a dull spot in the landscape? Once the purpose is defined, attention can then be given to colors and the number of plants.

Color use can vary from the simplest planting of a single color to a more complicated mix of colors. The first part of the design process is knowing the color wheel—violet, indigo, blue, green, yellow, orange, and red plus the colors in between (for example, red-orange, and so on). Colors can be mixed by using the colors adjacent to them on the spectrum such as yellow, yellow-orange, and orange or by using complementary colors that are opposites such as green and red.

Colors create feelings in a park. For example, red and yellow project a warm feeling. This combination is the most popular combination of colors in the world and has also become the symbol of spring, as in yellow daffodils with red tulips. Other combinations provide seasonal interest—such as red and green for winter holidays and yellow and bronze for the autumn. Shades of white, cream, off-white, and so on add elegance and sophistication to a landscape. Blues and pastels are cooler colors that blend well and complement green foliage. These colors must be used in larger masses, however, to be effective. Colors should harmonize and simplify the garden. Use colors in the red-to-blue or yellow-to-orange range for best results. Colors require care and thought before planting. Begin to use color in experimental plots and move the plants into the public areas as confidence in particular plants is gained.

Bright colors used in a garden reduce depth and should therefore only be used in the front of the garden. If that same color were used uniformly throughout the garden, no depth would be perceived even though the plant heights or textures might be different. While bright colors are best in the front of a garden, the cool colors such as purples, blues, and lavenders should be used in the garden's background. Depth in the garden can also be achieved by making sure that the large-leafed plants go in the background and plants with small leaves and delicate textures are up front where they can be fully appreciated.

There are two informal bed design styles:

1. The English border is 8 to 10 feet deep and much longer. The style (see Fig. 10.1) arranges individual or small groups of plants by height. The tallest, at the back, screens the background, while each succeeding lower plant screens the "legginess" of the taller plant behind it. The English border style is meant to be viewed from one side only and can use a wide variety of plants, colors, textures, and bloom periods. It requires strolling visitation for maximum appreciation of its beauty.

2. Island beds, more common in parks, flow gently in the landscape and usually contain trees, signs, large shrubs, and other mowing obstacles. The bed shape (see Fig. 10.2) consists of simple, smooth-flowing lines. The taller plants are in the center with low plants on the bed's edges (see Fig. 10.3). The wider the bed, the taller the plants in the center can be. Island beds are designed to be viewed from all sides. The plants should be grouped in numbers of five or more to avoid a formal appearance.

While mass plantings (see Fig. 10.4) will cover large areas of single species, combining single or small groups of plants in a garden requires a considerable knowledge of plant characteristics such as flower color, bloom period, plant height, leaf texture, and so on. Proper design will call for flower contrasts such as a mound of daisylike Black-Eyed Susans in bloom next to a large rock, as shown in Fig. 10.5. Heavy-textured Autumn Joy Sedum next to light-textured aster and large-leaf

Fig. 10.1

Fig. 10.2

hosta next to light and airy ferns can also be effective. Iris provide a nice vertical contrast to the horizontal vinca (see Fig. 10.6). The easiest way to make these matches is in the garden. By looking at plants in bloom at the same time, combinations of contrast and excitement can be moved around the garden. For example, pick some elegant Solomon's-Seal and put them into a vase in the garden to see how it looks next to brazen Oriental Poppies. If you like the look, mark it on your plan and do the transplanting later when the appropriate time of the year has come. Save the cut flowers for the kitchen table. Newly purchased plants can be kept in their pots in various barren locations until you find the right spot.

Proper design also calls for planting in groups of threes, such as one focal point or "star" plant and two "supporting" plants that improve the appearance of the

Fig. 10.3

Fig. 10.4

star. Consider planting in a star-to-supporting-plants ratio of 1:3, and plant in odd numbers such as one, three, five, seven, or nine plants to a group. Also consider the bed's background and use it in the garden design. For example, a pink or white geranium looks good against a red brick wall while plants with gray foliage such as artemisia and stachys look good with everything. White will provide dominance, and soft blue and lavender will be visible only to the observant gardener. Consider the textures of the garden's plants, rocks, benches, pavements, and so on. If a wall is brick, the path should also be brick. Bold-textured or spiked plants also provide a focal point. The iris in Fig. 10.7 provide a pleasing mix with the nearby bricks in the middle of the planting. Focal points give the observer a design they will feel comfortable with.

Fig. 10.5

Fig. 10.6

Some designers prefer to plant in drifts. Drifts of flowers have several plants at one end, and the planting area tapers down to a few plants at the other end. At the same time, an adjoining drift of flowers has a few plants that increase in number toward a wide planting at the far end. Modifications to this design can include clumps of other plants along the edge of drifts. Large drifts are more attractive than many small ones. Gaps of mulch should be left between the drifts.

Better Design Concepts

The city of Wellesley, Massachusetts, has implemented a flower planting program for many of its parklands, parking lots, public buildings, and memorials. Flowers

Fig. 10.7

are used to enhance the appearance of public areas and make them more enjoyable to Wellesley's residents and visitors. Attractive flowers are also used to draw attention to well-manicured parklands. Flowers are planted to supplement shrub plantings around public buildings and public parks and to beautify the public parking lots. Bulbs, as shown in Fig. 10.8, help to naturalize and "informalize" many parkland settings. They act as fillers for newly established shrub plantings and have been used to keep mowers at a safe distance from tree trunks. Other design examples include memorials planted with purple ageratum and red geraniums for Memorial Day celebrations.

Each year an average of 7500 flowers and bulbs are planted throughout the Wellesley community (see Fig. 10.9), and each year as well a large number of perennial flowers supplement a decreasing number of annuals. The perennials have life spans of several years, eliminating the need to plant annuals every year and therefore lowering costs. Figure 10.9 illustrates how the number of plants remains somewhat constant while the number of flower beds continues to grow as perennials replace annuals and better use is made of a given number of annuals. For example, one large bed contained a planting of 2000 ageratum in 1979. Today, those same 2000 plants go to several beds. Many beds contain small groupings, or in one case (see Fig. 10.10) several linear rows of annuals provide the illusion that an entire area has been mass planted. In fact, each plant becomes important as a focal point. Because mass planting is no longer affordable, this approach provides the same visual effect at a much lower cost.

Fig. 10.8

Management

Preparation of soil is the key factor in the development of a successful garden and landscape. The soil must provide nutrients and be friable so the soil will encourage vigorous growth for years to come. Construction and preparation of the soil is essential and usually requires a lot of hard work. However, the work is rewarded almost immediately with a successful garden.

Regardless of whether the area has been a garden previously or a garden of questionable quality, the preparation should be the same. It begins with an analysis of the existing soil, which will determine the soil's type and the amount of fertilizer, limestone, and organic matter required to bring the soil up to the optimum level. The soil should be analyzed to determine whether it is sand, which requires

WELLESLEY PARK AND TREE DIVISION

FLOWER PROGRAM

	ANNUALS	NUMBER OF PLANTS PERENNIALS	BULBS	TOTAL	ANNUALS	LABOR HOURS BULBS	BEAUTIFIED AREAS
1979	2,640		2,000	4,640	56	27	10
1980	3,322	90	3,450	6,862	80	46	18
1981	4,455			4,455	97	0	18
1982	3,100	25	2,000	5,125	76	27	15
1983	3,420	1,010	3,850	7,280	80	52	18
1984	3,040	1,010	2,850	6,900	75	38	16
1985	2,384 *320 2,704	1,030	1,791	5,525	141	24	30
1986	3,039 *1,392 4,431	1,199	4,350	9,980	188	62	40
1987	5,460 *1,088 6,548	1,141	4,723 * 620 5,343	13,032	291 * 10 301	66 * 6 72	49
1988	4,250 *1,152 5,402	477	5,190 * 725 *5,915	11,794	216 * 8 224	74 * 6 80	62
1989	4,350 *2,158 6,508	609	5,175 * 600 5,775	12,892	219 * 10 229	72 * 6 78	62
1990	77 *4,149 4,226	690	2,185 *1,240 3,425	8,341	157 * 13 170	41 * 6 47	63
1991	*2,660	8 * 175 183	2,450 * 900 3,350	6,193	93 * 13 106	40 * 6 46	63
1992	*2,695	78 * 80 158	3,325 * 500 3,825	6,678	94 * 13 107	52 * 4 56	63
1993	*2,876	56 * 132 188	3,625 * 700 4,325	7,389	107 * 13 120	56 * 5 61	65
1994	*3,176	29 * 135 164	2,940 *1,500 4,440	7,780	120 * 13 133	49 *15 64	66

*FLOWERS AND LABOR DONATED.

Fig. 10.9

extensive amounts of organic matter to create a loam (i.e., clay in need of sand and organic matter), or loam, which needs little improvement except organic matter.

Be sure the site has proper drainage. A raised bed may help correct drainage problems. The site should be leveled out and all weeds and grass growing on the bed should be removed. An ideal soil encourages deep roots and strong growth and has an ample supply of nutrients, moisture, and air. To create this ideal soil, a 4-inch layer of compost and/or peat should be rototilled into the top 12 inches of garden

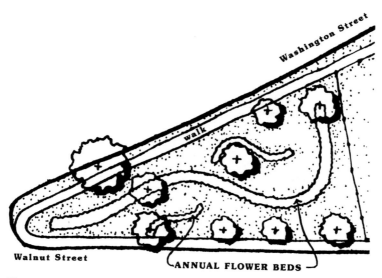

Fig. 10.10

loam. The compost can be sludge or mushroom compost, well-decomposed leaf mold, grass compost, or peat moss. If sand or additional compost is necessary, it should be added before planting. A 50 percent organic fertilizer such as 10-10-10 and 0-20-0 should also be added prior to or during planting (see Fig. 10.11). The fertilizer application rate should be 1 pound of nitrogen per 1000 square feet or 1 pound of 10-10-10 per 10,000 square feet. Because most flowering plants prefer a 5.5 to 6.8 pH, any corrections made to reach this level should also be made prior to planting. A generous mixture of organic matter is necessary to improve the soil structure and bind soil particles together. The optimum soil is 20 percent clay, 40 percent silt, and 40 percent sand and is known as loam. Loam is created by mixing sand, top soil, and compost in equal proportions. Loam will encourage the growth of microorganisms and earthworms, which continue to break down the organic matter so the plant can use them, while the worm holes provide soil aeration. Once the bed is completely prepared, it is ready for planting.

The final step prior to planting is the placement of the garden bed. Assuming the beds are properly tilled and prepared, the planting can begin. The edge of the bed can be laid out with a garden hose and then edged.

Planting

The planting of annuals and perennials should be done in the spring from the time the soil is dry enough to be worked until late May (July if irrigation is available). After the summer heat is over, perennial planting can resume until mid-October. Planting later than this may result in heaving from frost, which will not give the roots enough time to grow into the soil.

Fig. 10.11

The planting spaces should be as follows:

Small-growing plants: 8 to 12 inches apart (6 inches in mass plantings or four plants per square foot)

Intermediate-growing plants: 18 to 24 inches apart (15 inches in mass plantings)

Large-growing plants: 2 to 3 feet apart

All holes should first be dug a little larger than the root ball. A handheld auger is desirable for planting large numbers. Potted plants should be watered just before transplanting. Any bare root plants should be soaked in water or liquid fertilizer for a couple of minutes prior to planting. The roots of small tender plants should not be exposed to sunlight or drying wind for more than 30 seconds. Remove any plastic, metal, or clay pots. Papier-mâché, peat, or other organic containers need not be removed. Immediately after planting, the plants should be watered twice and then again every two days for two weeks. Thereafter, watering should be done deeply and once a week by rain or irrigation. Water the soil; do not water the leaves. A soaker hose is the best way to water around the leaves and directly on the soil.

Irrigation

To achieve maximum benefit with minimum effort, irrigation systems should always be automatic. Water sources require creativity. Consider using abandoned wells, surplus drainage water, groundwater with underground tanks acting as a reservoir, recycled water, gray water, special irrigation wells, and, as a last resort, drinking water. Moisture sensors will automatically bypass the controller if the ground has sufficient moisture. Be sure to check with the local irrigation supply companies to get the latest, most reliable sensor available. Moisture sensors are improving each year. Also consider drip irrigation (see Fig. 10.12) for shrub and flower beds as the latest, least expensive, and lowest-maintenance irrigation system available.

Mulching

Mulching can be done prior to planting if the mulch is pushed aside and spread back after planting. Other professionals prefer to add mulch after planting. An easy way to do this is to place the empty pot over the plant; after the mulch is added, the pot can be removed (see Fig. 10.13). This technique also keeps the mulch away from the plant stems, which can cause the plant to rot. The mulch material can be 2 inches of black, well-digested compost that has no weed seed and adds a rich appearance to the bed. This mulch is mixed into the soil every year if annuals are grown or supplemented with a fresh 1-inch layer in perennial beds. Other mulch materials that may be common in your area, such as shredded bark, buckwheat hulls, and so on, can also be used. A fine-textured mulch looks best in flower beds while a coarse mulch, such as corn cobs or wood chips, is good for trees and shrubs.

Advantages of Mulch

A good mulch should do the following:

Pull the design together with harmony

Suppress weeds

Provide color and texture to the landscape

Enhance the root development of all the plants

Fig. 10.12

Fig. 10.13

Add organic matter and nutrients to the soil through decomposition (although some nutrients are used in the decomposition process)

Improve water-holding capacity

Prevent water evaporation

Moderate soil moisture

Improve earthworm and soil insect growth, which moves organic matter into the soil

Improve aeration and

Encourage more root development into mulch and soil

Mulch should be applied to a settled depth of 3 inches for trees and shrubs, 1 inch for perennials, and 2 inches for annuals. Plastic is not a good mulch because it reduces soil oxygen and moisture and causes severe damage to plants after three years. Even in situations where the plastic has been covered with a mulch, after three years the roots will have surfaced in search of oxygen and moisture, and the plants will have become stressed.

Shade

Shade is defined as an area that has 3 hours or less of sun in a typical summer day. Partial shade or moderate shade has 3 to 6 hours of sun at a given spot, and a sunny site has more than 6 hours of sun exposure a day.

Because most annuals and perennials perform best in full sunlight, growing plants in the shade requires some moderate changes from the practices used to grow plants in the sun. The most obvious is plant selection. Many plants will tolerate shade, and they should be used in lieu of trying to grow sun-loving plants in the shade. Another change in practices involves soil moisture. Plants growing in the shade need less irrigation than those in the sun because the evaporation and transpiration rates are lower in shady areas than they are in the hot, dry, sunny spots. Plant growth rates tend to be slower in the shade because there is less sunlight for photosynthesis. Plants may therefore need to be planted closer together than those expected to grow rapidly in full sun. Some annuals that will tolerate shade include begonias, impatiens, nicotiana, periwinkle, and sweet alyssum. Some perennials that tolerate shade include barrenwort, primrose, foxglove, hosta, and sweet woodruff.

Plant Selection

It is very important to pick plants carefully. Some plants do very well in certain parts of the country but require extra care in other regions. There are many new varieties available that provide longer blooming periods, better colors, disease and pest resistance, and low maintenance needs. Check with local nurseries, read catalogs, and be aware of the latest in new plants. Recommended annuals and perennials are listed in Chap. 21, and detailed descriptions are provided in the Appendix.

Mass Plantings

Mass plantings are usually not affordable in the municipal park. For those situations where they are a necessary design element, mass plantings (such as those shown in Fig. 10.4) should at least be as maintainable as possible. Prior to planting, all of the soil should be prepared uniformly. All the plants must be uniform in variety and plant vigor. During the planting process, if any plant seems different from the rest, it should be pulled out. During planting, plants should also be planted with their leaves touching so no dirt is visible between them.

Plant selection is also important for keeping costs down. Begonias from seed are a lot less expensive than geraniums by the pot. The new plant varieties all seem to be genetically uniform in size, vigor, color, and growth requirements. Once you have found a successful selection, go with it.

Bright colors are also important in mass plantings. Almost all mass plantings are done with reds and oranges. The plants must be short and uniform in size. Foliage is not especially important unless it is the silvery-leafed plants used to form a border. Color should not be mixed in a mass planting bed. Even bicolored flowers looked speckled and uncomfortable in a large bed. Every successful mass planting garden has a test garden hidden from public view. This test garden not only provides a place to evaluate a few plants for next year, it also contains extra plants from this year's planting, "insurance" plants that can be dug up and put into the mass planting if something happens to some of the plants in the public display.

Perennials

Perennials need special care during the growing season. Staking of taller plants should be done when the plant is 6 inches high so the plant grows into and becomes a part of the stake. The stakes can be a single stake with twine, hoops and rings, linked stakes, or pea stakes. Staking after the bloom has broken is unattractive and, in any event, too late. The stakes should be removed with the flower stalk.

Many perennials also need to be divided every few years. This becomes necessary when the flowers are smaller or the plants have lost their vigor, are thick, are competing with each other, or are opening up in the center of the clump. The dividing process should begin when the plants are 3 to 4 inches tall. The plants are dug, and the soil is amended. The division is best done with two pitchforks placed back to back in the center of the plant. As the pitchforks are pushed against each other, the plant roots and stems separate into two new plants. Knife division takes longer and is not as good a method. Ornamental grasses are the exception and are best divided with a knife. Some plants that do well with division include iris, hosta, chrysanthemum, daylily, and astilbe. If the plants are doing well, leave them alone. Common Thrift is a plant that must be divided every three or four years. If it is not, a rot will develop in the center and spread to the whole clump.

Spring Bulbs

Most of the common spring bulbs such as daffodils and crocus provide bright colors and are very easy to grow. They will bloom for many years. They can be naturalized and should be considered a perennial for maintenance purposes. The naturalized planting style involves planting the bulbs in large masses and allowing them to multiply and flower naturally. They look good in clumps near the base of trees, mixed with perennials, and if planted in tall fescue grass meadows, they will greatly add to the site's natural appearance. Because of their clump characteristics, the fescues tend to be very compatible with bulbs. Figure 10.14 illustrates Fritillaria and Grape Hyacinth in a meadow. Spring bulbs are a very important part of the landscape. The only care that spring bulbs need is organic fertilizer placed in the hole at planting time. Bulbs will grow in any soil. Only in the worst of conditions, or when the bulbs are grown for show and must be perfect, must the bulbs be replaced annually.

Maintenance

Insects and diseases are seldom problems if resistant varieties are planted. Prevention of pests is best accomplished with sanitation, which includes cleaning up the garden in the fall. Insecticidal soap, Cleerys 3336, and dormant oil also prevent pests from reaching problem levels. When watering the garden, keep the hose or irrigation close to ground level to avoid wetting the foliage. Overhead watering is best done in the morning. Drip irrigation requires the least amount of maintenance and is the most efficient use of water. Keep in mind that flowering plants can easily be overwatered, especially if the soil contains a lot of organic matter.

If time permits, weed growth can be prevented by spraying perennial weeds with herbicide such as Roundup prior to bed construction and by applying an

Fig. 10.14

annual preemergent herbicide such as Surflan, Dacthal, or Trifluralin (Preen) in the spring. Deadheading is desirable to remove annual seed pods and dead flowers. Pinching some high-maintenance plants such as chrysanthemums early in the season keeps them low and bushy. Spring-flowering perennials should be pruned in half after flowering, while autumn-flowering perennials should be pinched in half in early summer. Winter damage is caused by dirt and salt covering the plants. Plants need to be washed off in the spring with rain or with laundry detergent and water-sprayed from a hydro-seeder or sprayer.

Downtown Plantings

The soil in downtown planting beds is very hostile to plants, and good planting sites are hard to find. New techniques are being introduced for the planting of bulbs and flowers. One excellent method being pioneered in Toledo, Ohio, requires plants and bulbs to be grown in 2-gallon pots. The plants are grown to maturity in a greenhouse and set, pot and all, into the flower bed rather than being planted in the soil (see Fig. 10.15). The pots of bulbs are easily replaced with pots of annuals, which in turn are easily replaced with pots of fall flowers. The pots eliminate the need to improve the planting bed soil. This technique creates an immediate effect and is less expensive than conventional planting. Weeding is much simpler with the pots and is done by hand. This innovative planting technique has greatly reduced the maintenance needs and vastly improved the aesthetics of downtown areas. Water needs do not change and must be attended to in the same manner as a conventional planting.

Contract Planting

Sometimes a contractor can be hired to assume all the responsibilities for growing and maintaining municipal flower beds. In downtown Detroit, Michigan, for example, specifications are written tightly and in great detail to ensure flower beds get exactly what is necessary to maintain proper growing conditions and maintenance. Irrigation systems are preferable to watering by the contractor because irrigation pays for itself in four to five years. It also results in a better quality product.

Fig. 10.15

The watering specifications are followed by the contractor and checked by the city. Soils available to the landscape contractor are usually junk, and the planting areas are specified to contain a new, total replacement soil of one-third compost, one-third sand, and one-third topsoil. All existing soil is excavated, and unless it is of extremely good quality it is removed. Because multiyear contracts are prepared, the annualized cost is lower since the biggest expense of preparing the initial bed is spread out over the period of the contract.

Rocky Soil

If you come from a region with rocky soil dealing with rocks is a major problem. Rocks are not desirable when preparing the planting bed and should be removed from the soil. There are a number of ways to deal with rocks and stones, other than to curse them, once they are extracted from the soil. The simplest and most common method is to dispose of them. On the other hand, if broken with a sledge hammer, rocks make a good, attractive mulch, and boulders are ideal for edging shrub and flower beds and holding the soil back in raised beds.

For alpine plants, large stones can be skillfully worked into a rock garden. They can be buried in a low area of the garden, used to line a dry well, or covered with soil or sod. Large stones can also be placed here and there in the park and garden as focal points. If you have enough large stones, you can build a wall.

As the Japanese teach us, rocks and stones of varying sizes because they are an integral part of nature can be worked into a number of attractive compositions with plants in the garden. Large handsome specimens can be positioned in the shade of large trees with ground covers such as lily of the valley, pachysandra, English ivy, and shade-loving wildflowers around them.

Small rocks can be set on sand and made into a very attractive garden path. After the walk is completed and has set for one season, moss should be planted because it will look good and will stabilize the stone path for many years to come. Small stones also make a very rich-looking gutter to control water runoff. In places where the gutter follows the edge of a park drive, small stones lend a certain feeling of richness while serving as a water control feature.

Figure 10.16 illustrates two plans for a rock garden planting. The planting plan is a top view of the proposed garden, and the elevation plan is a front view. Both of the plans had to work together to successfully complete this planting project. Figure 10.17 shows the right end of the garden while Fig. 10.18 shows the left side. Figure 10.19 shows the entire garden in the summer.

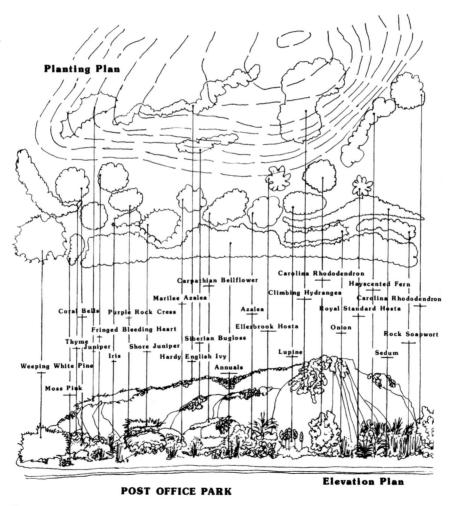

POST OFFICE PARK

Fig. 10.16

Fig. 10.17

Fig. 10.18

Fig. 10.19

References

DeSabato-Aust, Tracy, "Installation and Maintenance of Perennial Plants," *City Trees*, July/August 1993: 25–26.

McCarthney, Rob, "Installation and Maintenance of Annuals," *City Trees*, May/June 1993: 26.

Reinhold, Melanie, "Maintaining Downtown Plantings," *City Trees*, November/December 1988: 11.

Roche, Jerry, "Mixing Colors in the Landscape," *Landscape Management*, March 1994: 32, 34.

Stocker, Carol, "Pairings That Give a Garden Pizzazz," *Boston Globe*, May 13, 1993: A1.

Taloumis, George, "Rocks in the Landscape," *City Trees*, March/April 1987: 8.

Van der Hoeven, Gus, "Learn to Design Perennial Flower Gardens," *Grounds Maintenance*, April 1990: 102–106.

Yeager, Kenneth, "Downtown Plantings," *City Trees*, January/February 1991: 17.

11
Tree and Shrub Planting Techniques

Planting represents a major investment, and every effort should be made to ensure a tree or shrub the highest chance for survival. If a tree or shrub is to survive, it must be planted at the proper depth, be correctly pruned, and be watered and mulched.

Selection

How well a plant performs in the landscape depends on how well the plant is suited to the site in which it is to grow. The decision on the species selected should be based on the mature size of the tree or shrub. Can the site accommodate the roots at maturity? Is the soil the right type? Sun-loving plants should not be planted in the shade and vice versa. Tall trees should not be planted under utility wires, next to buildings, or within 20 feet of other tall trees. If 400 cubic feet of soil is not available to accommodate the root system, a tree should not be planted. If the site has poor drainage and it is not possible to correct it, the best alternative is to plant trees that will tolerate wet soils, such as Red Maple, Tupelo, London Plane Tree, Willow, Poplar, Willow Oak, Bald Cypress, and Basswood.

A quality tree or shrub is the best investment. Nursery-grown plants have been root pruned and are therefore more likely to survive a transplanting than plants dug from the woods. The root systems of nursery-grown plants are compact so more roots will accompany the tree or shrub during the transplanting. The number of roots left on the tree is critical to its survival. For bare root trees, a 2-inch caliper tree should have a minimum root spread of 32 inches. If the tree has a root ball, the ball diameter on the same size tree should be 24 inches and about 16 inches deep.

There is a tendency to plant young trees and shrubs close together for immediate visual impact. In the past, many planting programs emphasized close spacing, with as little as 20 to 30 feet between trees. Close spacing makes trees expensive to prune because the shade creates deadwood and branches that interfere with others. Spacing standards today (see Fig. 11.1) relate to the mature size of the species planted. For example, small shrubs are planted 5 feet apart while medium shrubs are placed 10 feet apart. Large shrubs and trees attaining a small mature size are planted a minimum of 25 feet apart; medium trees, 35 feet apart, and large trees, 55 feet apart.

The planting season will vary with the area, plant, and planting method. Experience and the advice of established nurseries and arborists in the region can provide these dates. Bare root trees are best planted when the leaves are off the trees. The best time is spring in northern or high-wind regions. Balled and burlapped (B & B) trees or trees grown in containers can be planted anytime the soil is workable and there is at least one month of growing season left for root development. Because most shrubs are container-grown or are B & B, they can also be planted anytime. Trees that form roots slowly in the spring and fall should only be planted in the spring. These include Oaks, Poplar, Tulip Tree, Hornbeam, Birch, Goldenrain Tree, evergreens, Maple, Magnolia, Zelkova, and Sourwood. Gingko and Ash generate roots equally fast in the spring and fall and can be planted either time. Linden and Yews generate roots more rapidly in the fall but can be planted in the spring or fall.

Design

The best chance of survival for trees and shrubs is through careful planning. When dealing with trees, planting the right tree in the right place is a theme heard frequently from experts. Plant hardy trees that withstand storms and the local environment. Plant trees and shrubs that fit the site and soil and avoid utilities. Don't

Fig. 11.1

plant tall shrubs that require pruning to keep them short, shallow-rooted trees next to sidewalks, or water-loving plants that require irrigation in dry areas.

The selection of plant material can be another big cost saver. For example, instead of planting ordinary and inexpensive Japanese or Chinese Yews that have to be pruned three or four times a year, plant English Spreading or Greenwave Yews, which maintain a height of 2 or 3 feet with a light pruning once every year or two. To avoid major cleanup costs, don't plant trees or shrubs that have thorns near sources of litter.

Transplanting large trees is often considered essential to achieving a design that looks mature. However, during the digging process, many roots are cut off. Root replacement can take up to five years on a 4-inch tree, and on a 10-inch tree 12 years will be needed to restore its root development. Large trees should therefore be moved for immediate effect and design purposes only. For tree vigor, the smaller, the better.

Transplanting

Trees and shrubs can be transplanted in four different ways of varying size and cost. The most commonly selected form is *balled and burlapped* (B & B). Brown plastic and green artificial burlap should always be removed at planting time. Brown natural burlap, however, can be rolled down and left around the base of the ball. This should decay in six weeks. Survival by B & B transplanting is usually 90 percent or higher, even though only 5 percent of the tree's roots are moved with the tree.

The second most often used form of transplanting trees and shrubs up to 3 inches in trunk diameter is bare root. *Bare root* (B.R.) trees may have more roots than B & B trees, but they also have fewer surviving root hairs, which are needed to ensure planting success. B.R. plants are dug while dormant and are kept in cold storage over winter. Care must be taken to prevent the trees and shrubs from drying out and to ensure that they are kept dormant and below 45° Fahrenheit prior to planting. B.R. trees and shrubs must be planted as soon as possible after delivery to ensure a high survival rate. If planting is not possible, they should be healed in or kept dormant, cool, and moist. The survival rate can vary from 60 to 90 percent of the transplants.

Container-grown trees and shrubs are excellent for small- to medium-sized stock. Containerized plants can be planted anytime the ground is not frozen or in drought. Care should be taken when planting that the roots do not encircle the container. Those that have should be loosened. Some roots should be extended out and into the backfill to encourage rapid plant establishment. One hundred percent of the tree's roots are growing in the container so the chances of survival after planting are nearly 100 percent. Unfortunately, not all varieties will do well in containers.

The final transplanting techniques to be discussed are for large trees. The tree spade saves a lot of labor and allows trees to be moved almost anytime during the growing season. Caution should be used to be sure the tree is not too large for the spade and not too many roots are cut by the blades. The spade can also glaze the soil, especially if there is a high clay content. Glazing retards root penetration from the root ball into the surrounding soil, but this problem can be corrected by roughening the sides of the hole prior to planting. The survival rate will vary considerably, and five years is not even enough time to ensure survivability.

Soil Preparation

Experiments have shown that root growth in plain soil is neither different nor better than in a soil with amendments such as peat, perlite, or sawdust. If the planting soil is all rubble, the planting site should be abandoned or new soil should be brought in. If the planting soil requires drainage, it should be corrected. Excessive peat moss in the planting hole, however, will act like a sponge and cause the tree or shrub to drown. Soil amendments also encourage a fibrous root ball that does not extend into the surrounding soil so that once the improved planting hole is filled with roots the tree begins to decline. Soils as poor as that shown in Fig. 11.2 are still better for tree and shrub growth without amendments.

Hole Preparation

According to the latest research reported by American Forests (the association) trees and shrubs survive better if planted in a large planting area such as the area shown in Fig. 11.4 than in a planting hole like the one shown in Fig. 11.3: that is, wide but not deep, with soil that is loose and suited for root growth. Such planting areas should be five times the diameter of the planting ball. A rototiller or shovel should be used to loosen the soil throughout the area to a depth of about 12 inches. Organic matter can be added to the loosened soil so long as the new material is mixed uniformly throughout the large area.

Fig. 11.2

Planting

In the center of the prepared area, a shallow hole should be dug in which the tree or shrub will be set. The proper planting depth is the point where the flare of the trunk meets the roots. The hole should allow the root ball to sit on solid ground rather than on loose soil. Once the ball is set in the hole, its

Fig. 11.3

upper surface should be level with the existing soil. The plant should be removed
from its container along with all rope, wire, and artificial burlap. Position the plant
so it is vertical and its branches will not cause harm to pedestrians or any abutter.
Once it is set in the hole, the soil should be added gradually.

For bare root plants, work the soil firmly at the base of the roots. Then add more
soil and work it under and around the lower roots. The plant may be raised and
lowered gently during the filling process to eliminate air pockets and bring the
roots in close contact with the soil. When the roots are just covered, add water, let
the soil settle, and finish filling the hole with loose soil. Since a root hair is exposed

Fig. 11.4

to wind and sun every 30 seconds, cutting the survival rate by 50 percent, keep roots out of the ground for as short a period of time as possible.

Planting by B & B or container follows the same method, including using water to settle the soil against the ball. After the filling is completed, rake a 4-inch dike to form a saucer around the circumference of the planting hole (see Fig. 11.5). The saucer will hold water and prevent runoff for a while after planting. Also be sure the plant is 1 inch higher than the height it grew to in the nursery.

Management

Trees and shrubs require a long-term commitment to proper management. Management must be comprehensive and cover a wide range of maintenance activities. However, giving a plant, tree, or shrub proper care early and often will reduce the care needed as it matures.

In every new construction project, the person responsible for the landscape maintenance should make every effort to have input with the person creating the design. The plans should be checked for maintenance-saving improvements and to be sure there are provisions for maintenance and service equipment. When dealing with open space maintenance, evaluate all open space lands through a master plan design process to review maintenance needs and get an overview of maintenance requirements.

Pruning

When B & B trees or shrubs are being transplanted, only 4 or 5 percent of the roots are taken along. Excessive pruning to compensate for the root loss is considered harmful because the plant's ability to make food in its leaves is reduced. It is better to keep the roots well watered and growing than to remove the leaves from the plant.

Before planting, check over the plant to remove all sucker growth and all dead, broken, damaged, or weak branches and roots. All girdling roots should also be removed. Two or three years after planting, determine the desired shape of the plant by pruning to correct structural weakness, removing the lower branches if necessary, and prune to the ideal shape, branching habit, and a single leader. Studies have proved that pruning young trees

Fig. 11.5

is better for the tree: the wounds are smaller, and properly pruned young trees need less pruning as the trees get older.

Watering

Water absorption in newly transplanted trees or shrubs is limited because so few of the roots are present. When a tree or shrub is planted, the hole should be filled with water when halfway done and again when it is completely planted. The saucer should be filled two more times within 24 hours after planting. Even if it is raining, a thorough watering will eliminate trapped air pockets and reduce transplant shock. After planting, a thorough watering once a week is necessary until the end of the growing season. On extremely hot or windy days, a very fine misting of the leaves may be necessary several times a day. Watering may also be necessary during drought periods for a few years after planting.

Fertilizing

Only 5 percent of the roots survive the transplanting and are available to absorb fertilizer. It is therefore better to hold off on fertilizing when planting. Once new leaves have matured, a light fertilizing can be performed. Too much nitrogen fertilizer will push leaf development at a rate faster than the roots can support. However, phosphorus "starter" fertilizer will help root development. A pH of 6.5 to 7.0 is also desirable for maximum root development. Once the plants are established, a slow-release 10-10-10 or 20-20-20 fertilizer plus 2 to 4 inches of mulch will encourage plant vigor. Slow-release fertilizer packets can be used during the planting because the plants will only be able to use the fertilizer once the roots have grown toward it.

Finishing Touches

Trees do not need to be wrapped. Wrapping slows the tree's ability to adapt to a new site. Wrapping tape also provides a habitat for insects, and the string holding the wrap can girdle the tree. If a tree comes from the nursery with a wrapped trunk, remove it during the planting (as shown in Fig. 11.6).

Trees should not be staked unless wind is a problem or the tree develops a lean. Trunk movement is necessary for building trunk strength so trees should be supported with a flexible stake or guy wire that will keep the trunk straight. If used, all stakes and guy wire should be removed between 12 and 18 months after planting.

Mulch

Mulch should be spread in the plant saucers. The mulch can be any locally available product that will simulate the natural conditions of the forest floor. The mulch should let moisture and air enter the soil and eliminate the competition from weeds. Most importantly, it keeps mowers and string trimmers away from the trunk. Mowers and trimmers cause more trees to decline and die than anything

Fig. 11.6

else in the urban landscape. Mulch that is more than 4 inches deep will smother the tree roots. The mulch decomposition rate should be checked annually and new mulch added if necessary. Mulch protects new as well as larger trees from mowers and trimmers (see Fig. 11.7). Mulch is also desirable in shrub beds (see Fig. 11.8).

Follow-Up

If a plant should die, care should be taken to determine the cause before another is planted. If poor drainage is a problem, it should be corrected. If vandalism is a

Fig. 11.7

Fig. 11.8

problem, have neighborhood kids help plant a new tree or shrub. Also add a large stake (5 feet tall) beside the plant to help protect it for its first two years.

Shrubs

At the present time, shrubs have not been a very popular gardening item in the 1990s. They are still used in the landscape, however, and some of them, such as Junipers, Forsythia, and Yews, are even used to excess. Other shrubs are avoided, perhaps because there are too many varieties of shrubs, such as Viburnum and Azalea. Shrubs lack the stature of trees, the vigor and color of annuals, and the glamour of flowering plants. Their popularity has waned in favor of ornamental grasses and low-maintenance flowering perennials, and they are often the overlooked, mistreated, and a misunderstood segment of the landscape. When the annual All-American Selections are made, new varieties seldom include shrubs. Nurseries offer one new shrub a year versus 10 new trees and 50 new annuals and perennials. In the public landscape, shrubs are the plants behind which drug dealers and sex offenders hide, and consequently they are often cut down. In the private landscape, the shrub is used in the front yard because it is easily sheared, cut back, and taken for granted. Shrubs are always considered last. They get the leftover spaces and are always left to fend for themselves.

Despite their poor reputation, however, shrubs are a vital part of the landscape. With care, their performance is greatly enhanced, and they will often grow and take abuse where nothing else will succeed. There are by some accounts over 2000 species and varieties of shrubs that are worthy of planting in parks around the country.

In order to begin to use shrubs in the landscape, consideration must be given first to their bloom period. When does it occur in relation to other shrubs? Are the colors harmonious with others? The next consideration concerns the shrub's size. Its mature size is a most important factor for park use and reduced maintenance. Planting a yew that grows to be 10 feet tall but keeping it pruned to 3 feet is a wasted effort. Transplant that larger yew to another location where it can be allowed to grow to its full height, and plant a lower growing yew in its place. The shrub's size is also a consideration in a park's design. Ground covers or low shrubs are useful as hedges, as foundation plantings, and as screens in front of larger shrubs.

Foliage is another major factor when considering the use of shrubs. Most shrubs are green during the growing season. The exceptions might be variegated leaves with white-, cream-, or red-colored patterns or the yellow leaves of shrubs like Golden Ninebark. The beauty of autumn color in shrubs is second only to that of trees—the intense red of Euonymous alatus (Burning Bush) is an example. Fragrant flowers are very popular in places where people can sit and enjoy the shrubs. Many shrubs also have fragrant leaves, but their scent is only evident if the leaves are crushed. Junipers are an excellent example of shrubs with fragrant leaves, while Fragrant Viburnum (V. carlesii) and Summersweet (Clethra alnifolia) are also noted for their very fragrant flowers.

Shrubs are also very useful for special purposes. Some will grow in harsh conditions of poor soil or hot sun while others will grow in the shade or in wet soil. Still others tolerate salt, acid soil, very cold climates, and urban conditions.

Many shrubs have special uses. Those with rapid root growth or stolons are good for steep sites or for preventing erosion. Those with thorns are useful as barrier plants. Many evergreen shrubs provide screens and windbreaks with year-round value. Deciduous hedges are especially useful in the growing season but only partially useful during winter. One advantage shrubs have over trees is that their interesting bark is low enough so that it can be appreciated. Many shrubs have exfoliating bark that either shreds in long strips or flakes off in patches. The bark of shrubs also has a great deal of color variation, from the gray of the Gray Dogwood (Cornus racemosa) to the red of red-stemmed dogwood (Cornus alba), the green of Kerria japonica, and the brown or black of most other shrubs.

References

Bassick, Nina, and Pat Lindsey, "The Urban Jungle," *Grounds Maintenance,* June 1991: 11.

Baumgardt, Dr. John P., "GM Guide to Planting a Tree," *Grounds Maintenance,* October 1975: 38.

Boerner, Deborah A., "Nurturing New Trees," *Urban Forests,* July/August 1990: 6.

Cinque, Marie T., "Precautions for Digging and Transplanting Out of Season," *Weeds, Trees and Turf,* August 1979: 46.

Harris, Dr. Richard W., "Early Care of Trees in the Landscape, *American Nurseryman,* September 15, 1976: 14.

Miller, Dr. Robert W., *Urban Forestry, Planning & Managing Urban Greenspaces,* Englewood Cliffs, NJ: Prentice Hall, 1988.

Moll, Gary A., "The Best Way to Plant Trees," *Urban Forests,* March/April 1990: 8.

Patterson, Dr. James C., "Soil and Design Considerations," *City Trees,* January/February 1991: 12.

Phillips, Leonard E., "Solution to the Greenhouse Effect," *City Trees,* January/February 1989: 4.

————, "Tree Bracing Collars," *City Trees,* April 1986: 6.

"Researching Maintenance" (column), *Grounds Maintenance,* August 1991: 1.

Watson, Dr. Gary, "Disorders Caused by Root Related Stresses," *City Trees,* September/October 1990: 15.

Whitcomb, Carl E., "Factors Affecting the Establishment of Urban Trees," *Journal of Arboriculture* 5, no. 10 (October 1979): 217–219.

12

Xeriscaping and Mesiscaping

What are xeriscaping and mesiscaping? Xeriscaping is landscaping that involves using plants that demand lower but equal quantities of water. For example, if seven plants are required for a design, the xeriscape design approach would mean that all seven plants would require less water than an alternative and that the water requirements for all seven plants would be the same. Xeriscaping is useful for areas such as the western half of the United States where moisture loss is great, and it is especially desirable for traffic islands (see Fig. 12.1) anywhere in the United States where the surrounding pavement creates a great deal of summer heat and water absorption is limited. Xeriscaping can also be beneficial for home landscapes, where it is estimated that 40 to 50 percent of the annual average water consumption goes to lawns and gardens. Xeriscape principles help to conserve water, which saves money, and they can also reduce maintenance needs if low-maintenance and xeriscape plants are used.

The term *xeriscape* comes from *xeros,* which is Greek for dry, and was coined in Denver in the 1980s in response to the difficulty of growing plants with a diminishing supply of water. A task force met to establish a program of water conservation for the green industry. From this task force grew a better definition of xeriscaping: water conservation through creative landscaping. From 1986 to 1993, the National Xeriscape Council was the umbrella organization for all the xeriscape programs across the United States. It coordinated information, distributed literature, and promoted xeriscape demonstration projects in various communities around the country. The Council had members in most states and projects from coast to coast. Unfortunately, the Council did not achieve financial stability and failed.

Fig. 12.1

The term *mesiscape* comes from *mesic,* which means moderately moist and describes the climate of the extreme West Coast and the eastern half of the United States, where rainfall exceeds 30 inches per year. Mesiscaping uses a wider range of plants than xeriscaping, which utilizes only the plants that are typical of the western deserts and other locations where rainfall is less than 30 inches a year. The mesiscape approach combines low maintenance, organic gardening methods, and adaptable plants. In this chapter, both terms will be used interchangeably.

Xeriscape Design Principles

Xeriscape design consists of seven basic principles: (1) to provide professional planning and design in order to allow for the proper location and selection of plants; (2) to reduce turf areas to only those essential areas where it is functionally beneficial and to replace the grass with less water-demanding materials; (3) to use irrigation only as needed and according to plant needs; (4) to improve the soil to increase its water-holding capacity; (5) to use all types of organic and inorganic mulches as much as possible; (6) to use less water-demanding plants such as ground covers or ornamental grasses; and (7) to provide regular and appropriate maintenance to preserve the intent and beauty of the xeriscape planting.

The first and most important step in redesigning an existing landscape into a xeriscape landscape is to significantly reduce the area of turf. This is accomplished by removing turf under trees. In sloped areas, turf is a major maintenance problem, and undulating areas are also difficult to maintain in a uniform condition. If the high spots are moist, the swales are soggy. If ground covers and plants with aggressive root systems are used instead of turf in these areas, maintenance costs are reduced and the landscape's appearance is improved. Consider replacing turf with shrub beds, wildflower areas, and large mulched areas. Native plants or cultivars of native plants should be used as much as possible. Native plants will have a higher degree of adaptability, pest resistance, naturalness of appearance, and suitability to local water availability than will exotic plants. Cultivars and hybrids of native plants have been developed to have higher pest resistance or better flower or leaf display than native plants. Remember that native plants will do best in native soil, and because few U.S. cities still have native soil, exclusive use of native plants is unnecessary.

The following criteria should be considered when designing an area using xeriscape principles:

1. Determine how adaptable the chosen species are to the soils of the site.
2. Consider whether shallow roots will raise paving and curbs or whether the roots will outcompete other shallow-rooted plants.
3. Determine whether the selected plants are resistant to pests and diseases.
4. Find out if the selected plant combination is going to result in competitive growth rates.
5. Determine if narrow strips, hard-to-maintain corners, and isolated islands of grass have been adequately avoided.
6. Concentrate plants with the greatest water and energy needs at a location that will provide maintenance attention.
7. Keep low water consuming plantings separate from those requiring conventional irrigation to facilitate the design of the irrigation system.
8. Design and install the irrigation system at the same time as the landscape design.
9. Apply water more slowly to slopes than to flat surfaces.
10. Use a drip system to irrigate low water demand areas. Consider minisprinklers in other areas.
11. Ensure that drip and spray systems are zoned separately.
12. Ensure that native or ornamental grass varieties are on different irrigation zones than turf grass.
13. Use deep-root watering devices to water trees and high water demand shrubs.
14. Use shade trees to reduce water evaporation in the hot sun.
15. Irrigate turf areas only when and where needed.
16. Develop wind barriers with tall plants, evergreens, or fences.

Given that southern and western exposures will have heat and water losses and different evaporation rates, plants for such locations should be selected accordingly. Plants near buildings and paved surfaces will also be stressed by heat and drought. A common cause of plant failure is the combining of plants that will not tolerate the same irrigation frequency on a common site. Most urban soils are highly compacted so success in these sites requires careful plant selection as well as good irrigation design and excellent installation procedures. Plants should be selected that have common low-maintenance needs and are nonevasive.

The need to select plant species that match the soil conditions and achieve water savings narrows the plant palette in direct relation to the severity of any soil problems. Fortunately, there are many new and seldom used old plants available that are adaptable to xeriscapes as well as to the poor soil sites so commonly seen in American cities.

General plant lists are not recommended because almost every plant will tolerate dry soil provided other soil conditions and the site are appropriate for that particular plant. Xeriscaping requires that consideration of such factors be made during the design process and before planting. When trees are planted at a site, the air flows, temperature, shade, radiation, and the like around a structure can all be affected. Xeriscaping also requires that soil improvements be made to improve the site for plant materials. Plants should be carefully sited so that all the water demands in an area are similar. High water demanding plants can be used in a low water garden if they are planted in low spots where runoff collects. Watering with soaker hoses, drip irrigation, or bubblers is more efficient than using a sprinkler system. Practicing good maintenance of the plants will also reduce water needs.

Management

There are a large number of low water demanding plants available for use that can produce a visually attractive landscape. There are also many varieties of perennials, shrubs, and dryland grasses that can be planted to provide a range of color and texture. Local nurseries and gardening experts can supply this information to municipal officials. All of the perennials recommended in the Appendix are considered low-maintenance plants that will do well in locations with at least 30 inches of rainfall a year.

People

Why should we worry about saving water? According to the American Association of Nurserymen, "In the United States in 1984, 82 billion gallons of water were taken from ground water supplies each day, and only 61 billion gallons were replaced through rain or runoff—a daily deficit of 21 billion gallons. The problem is real. It is acute. It is permanent and long-range solutions must be found." Another study showed that 40 to 50 percent of annual average residential water use and costs go for lawn and garden watering. This is equivalent to 90,000 gallons of water per house per year. Substantial water savings of 30 to 80 percent can result from the implementation of better water conservation landscape designs. Professionals wishing to contribute to water conservation can implement xeriscapes in the design of new projects and the retrofitting of old projects. A site's microclimate should be examined and utilized so that, for example, wet, shady sites will not contain plants that will only grow in hot and dry sites.

Water conservation is an issue all over the globe. Trees, shrubs, and flowers are our natural heritage and can play an important role in conserving water and energy.

References

American Association of Nurserymen, "The Impact of Bans of Watering Landscape Plants," Washington: American Association of Nurserymen, 1982.

Coate, Barrie, "Xeriscape: Dry and Beautiful," *Agora*, fall 1985: 11–15.

Latta, Martha, "Designing for Water Conservation," *City Trees*, September/October 1990: 14.

Stoud, Teresa, "Xeriscaping—Xeri-What?" *Grounds Maintenance*, April 1987: 74–82.

13

Ornamental Grasses

There is a whole new type of grass appearing in the American landscape. In fact, it can be found in successful gardens throughout the world. This grass, which is meant to be unmowed and untrimmed, is collectively called ornamental grass. A complete description of available ornamental grasses is presented in Chap. 22.

Design

Ornamental grasses are very informal in appearance and can be described as soft, elegant, and graceful. They fit into any garden, park, and commercial or institutional setting (see Fig. 13.1). Their use is limited only by the site. There are grasses that are uniform in appearance and can be used as a hedge in a formal garden (see Fig. 13.2), and grasses that resemble primitive wilderness grass. A few other grasses can be used selectively with rocks and mosses in a low-maintenance, naturalistic garden to present the appearance that they are attempting to grow in a very harsh environment (see Fig. 13.3).

Grasses with fine texture need to be located against a plain wall in order for their blooms to be seen. Large specimens need to be very carefully located as a focal point. When several grasses are used together, their textural differences as well as their heights should be considered. Fine textures (as seen in Fig. 13.4) should go in front of coarse textures. The movement of their leaves and flowers as well as their seasonal changes and year-round colors should be used to advantage in the garden. When most other plants have died back, the late fall and winter sizes of ornamental grasses can also be exploited to great advantage in the public garden.

Fig. 13.1

Fig. 13.2

Fig. 13.3

Fig. 13.4

Grasses are low-maintenance plants intended to appear loose and flowing. They give the garden the natural look of fields or prairie. They are useful in naturalized areas, edges, ground covers, and rock gardens, and as accent plants. Their clump appearance can be quite dramatic. They are best used in combination with low-maintenance annuals and perennials where grasses become the focal plant (see Fig. 13.5).

Management

The summer growth of ornamental grass is rapid and quickly achieves mature height. In the fall, the blooms appear. In the winter, when these grasses are in their

Fig. 13.5

dormancy their tan leaves and blooms can still be appreciated, and their foliage and plumes are useful and attractive in flower arrangements as fresh or dried flowers. They are ideal for long-lasting bouquets. In the spring, the old leaves and dried blooms are removed prior to new growth. Ornamental grasses are divided into two climate groups—warm-temperature grasses and cool-temperature grasses, or approximately zones 7 through 10 and zones 5 through 9 of the U.S. Department of Agriculture's latest hardiness zone map (Fig. 22.1 on page 184). Some ornamental grasses thrive in dry sites while others are suited to wetter sites. Most are suited to well-drained sites.

The maintenance requirements of ornamental grasses are quite simple. The spring cleaning takes the most time and effort. The plants are resistant to most diseases and insect attacks, and the appropriate fertilizer is the same as perennials get, applied when the perennials are fertilized. Ornamental grasses have long, deep roots, so watering is generally not needed, and they tend to be heat-resistant. In general, ornamental grasses are very long-lived plants. They prefer sunny locations and rich loam soil but will tolerate poor soil and in fact will improve it.

Ornamental grasses come in many varieties, and their colors, textures, and sizes vary with each variety. Their foliage is as striking as those of flower spikes (see Fig. 13.6). A list of currently available ornamental grasses is provided in Chap. 22. These plants should be considered for new plantings but can also be used as accents in existing plantings.

Fig. 13.6

References

Ottesen, Carole, *Ornamental Grasses— The Amber Wave,* New York: McGraw-Hill, 1989.

14

Turf Management

For the grounds manager, turf care is critical and represents the most important part of the park's maintenance operations. Parks with poor turf quality look bad and create a bad impression of you and your staff. Proper turf care is easy as long as you know what to do. An easily followed program is presented in this chapter. If followed closely, it will result in a better-looking lawn that uses less water and fertilizer and fewer herbicides, insecticides, and fungicides.

Soil

The condition of the soil is very important for the survivability of turf grass. The soil should be loose, fertile, and moist. Using good soil at the start is as important as proper maintenance in all the years that follow. The soil should be a loam that has been properly prepared, and it should contain at least one-third compost, one-third sand, and one-third topsoil. It should be properly prepared by tilling or mixing deep into the subsoil. There should be at least 4 to 6 inches of topsoil, and the bed should be prepared by removing all twigs, rocks, and roots. Lime and fertilizer should be added as necessary based on soil test results.

Fertilizer

Athletic fields should receive an annual average of 4 pounds of nitrogen per 1000 square feet of soil. The nitrogen should be applied at the rate of 1 or 2 pounds three times a year: once between May 15 and June 15 to prolong the rapid spring growth; during September to recover from summer heat and stress; and a single or double dose in mid-November to encourage root growth and keep the grass green well into the fall. If any fertilizing is skipped, it should be the September application. Soil tests on the site are essential to indicate deficiencies and to ensure a balance between nitrogen and phosphorus. The nitrogen-phosphorus ratio should be 2:1. Overfertilizing will promote excessive growth and turf disease, and underfertilizing will encourage weed growth and plant mortality.

Try to use a quality fertilizer product such as a 20-10-10 granular fertilizer with a 50 percent urea-form organic nitrogen. The organic base will prevent burning and overstimulation while providing a slow release of nutrients. The inorganic base provides the immediate response typical of liquid and inexpensive fertilizers. The granular fertilizer will allow for a uniform distribution of the nutrients using a fertilizer spreader such as the tractor-mounted model shown in Fig. 14.1. The granules contain quick-release ingredients on the surface and slow-release ingredients in the center. This provides for a long period of nutrient release and allows for extended periods of time between fertilizer applications.

Liquid fertilizer was a very popular option in the 1980s. It can, however, stick to the grass blades and then be cut off before the nutrients can be fully utilized. This problem is somewhat less of a concern however, if the clippings are not collected. Regardless of the method chosen to get fertilizer to the grass plant, the fertilizer must get deep into the soil so the plant's roots can absorb the nutrients.

Biostimulants

Biostimulants improve turf's vigor and disease resistance while providing additional plant hormones that enhance growth. The two biostimulants are cytokinin

Fig. 14.1

and triazole. The most popular source of biostimulants is seaweed extract. Bio-stimulants enhance rooting, which improves drought resistance, salt tolerance, and plant color and reduces nutrient requirements. During periods of plant stress, grasses use up their natural hormones, and this outside source of hormones provides visible and positive results. Biostimulants can be applied alone, with fertilizer, or with iron.

Broadleaf Weed Control

The best way to control dandelions and other common weeds is to keep grass healthy. Certain weeds are indicative of poor soil conditions. For example, clover in the grass means more nitrogen is needed; sheep sorrel indicates acidity; knotweed and goosegrass thrive in gravel or compacted soil; quack grass and yarrow mean the soil needs loosening and more organic material; and algae and mosses mean acidity, excessive shade, or mowing too close. Once these poor conditions are corrected and the lawn areas reseeded, weeds should not be a major problem. If there are a lot of weeds or areas of unhealthy grass, use a product with fertilizer and broadleaf weed control once instead of the May-June fertilizer application. After this single treatment or if there are only a few weeds in the lawn, use a liquid broadleaf weed control mixed according to the label instructions and spot treat the biggest weeds. Using this approach, major weed control will only be necessary every five years or so. Repeated applications of herbicide several times a year, year after year, weaken the grass plants and add unnecessary herbicide to the environment.

Crabgrass Weed Control

Any preemergent crabgrass control product can be used but should only be used if crabgrass was a major problem the previous summer. Preemergent material should be applied at the same time the forsythia are in bloom. Again, if the grass is healthy, crabgrass should not be a concern, and unnecessary herbicide should not be applied.

pH Modification

To keep the grass growing well, the soil chemistry should be in balance. A soil test will provide this information. Apply lime to balance the soil pH according to the test results and recommendations. Lime applications should also be alternated between calcite and dolomitic limestone to provide a balance of nutrient by-products and minor elements. Soils with a pH of 6.5 or higher should be supplemented with sulfur to lower the pH rate. Because sulfur also affects soil drainage and soluble salts will increase, it should be applied only when absolutely necessary. Aeration and wetting agents applied in conjunction with a sulfur treatment will reduce these problems.

Grass Seed

If you are redoing a lawn or filling in bare spots with new seed, use a high-quality blend of grass seed that contains some new varieties of grass suited for your region. There are several new varieties that require little water, are disease-resistant, and are not bothered by insects such as chinch bugs. These grasses are usually compatible with the grasses growing in your region. The grass seed should have high germination levels and low weed and inert matter levels. The seed should be applied at the proper rate for the grass species. A complete description of turf grasses has been provided in Chap. 23.

Do not add seed at the base of trees. In fact, if possible, all the grass should be removed to provide a 2- to 3-foot-diameter mulched saucer around all tree trunks to prevent lawn mower damage. Most of the dead trees on lawn areas are killed by mowers or grass trimmers banging into and damaging the inside of the tree trunks. Often the damage is not even visible, and the cause of the tree's death is not even known until it is too late.

Sodding

Sodding is an alternative to seeding that provides an instant lawn and immediate soil stabilization. It is five to eight times more expensive than seeding but is often required if quick establishment of a turf is necessary. Sod needs irrigation and proper bed preparation just like seed. Care should be taken during sodding to be sure the sod is kept moist and lightly rolled after it is laid. The irrigation program should be monitored to keep it at the 1-to-1-½-inch a-week level. Thickly cut sod will need less water, but the time to knit the sod to the soil will be longer. Sod should be locally grown, and freshly cut the previous day if possible. The less the sod is exposed to sun and wind, the faster it will knit to the soil. It should be stored in shade prior to being installed.

When using sod, be sure the grass varieties in the sod are suitable for your site. As with seed, be sure the sod is certified. Ask the grower if herbicides or fertilizers have been applied to the sod recently: you could overdose without knowing what happened. Sprigging and stolonizing can also be used to establish a turf. Both of these options cost less than sod but more than seed, and both establish turf faster than seed while requiring more labor. Both options are used only where financial and special site conditions warrant them. Experienced labor and special equipment is required for success with either of these techniques.

Hydroseeding

Using a hydroseeding or hydraulic planting machine to plant grass seed can often speed up the planting process. After the seed bed is properly prepared, the hydroseeder applies a mat of seed, fertilizer, mulch, and water that creates an environment suitable for seed germination. The mat can be a mulch material made of wood fiber, shredded paper, chopped cardboard, or paper mill sludge. The use of a tackifier, which is a powered organic glue, is also necessary in the mix to hold the mat in place, especially when it is applied on steep slopes. Seed and fertilizer requirements are the same as those described earlier in this chapter. Lime, gypsum, sulfur, and other soil amendments such as sludge or organic material can also be applied to the soil hydraulically.

The entire mix is prepared by adding all the ingredients to the hydroseeder tank. The hydroseeder must provide constant mixing action to prevent the ingredients from settling in the tank. The mix is sprayed over the site as uniformly as possible. If a contractor is supplying the materials and doing the hydroseeding, be sure to check that the ingredients and number of bags per tank are applied at the specified coverage. Hydroseeding equipment is expensive and requires knowledge of the special techniques used to operate the equipment properly. Only the most talented crews and the larger park departments should consider hydroseeding themselves.

Aeration

Thatch is a layer of dead roots that indicates unhealthy turf. The thatch layer is found on top of the soil. If more than ½-inch thick, this layer will prevent nutrients and water from reaching the healthy grass roots. Instead of removing the thatch with a thatching machine every spring, punch deep holes in the soil with an aerator three times a year: spring, summer, and late fall. Aerating loosens the compact soil, allows the soil and grass roots to breathe, and lets moisture and fertilizer penetrate deeper. If plugs are removed by the aerator, they should be taken away, chopped, and dragged back into the turf depending on the soil conditions. Fertilizing should follow aeration. Combined with proper turf care, fertilizing will prevent thatch from becoming a problem. Mow the grass once a week, or more often if possible, and leave the clippings on the ground. They will quickly fall between the live grass plants and decompose within two weeks, returning many nutrients to the soil.

Thatch is not always bad. If a thatch layer is less than ½-inch thick it can act as a shock absorber on turf. This prevents soil compaction from being as severe as it might otherwise be if there were no thatch at all. Some thatch also prevents the loss of moisture from the soil.

Water

The ideal amount of water for turf is 1 inch per week. If it rains, for example, ½ inch during the week, add another ½ inch with irrigation. Long watering periods penetrate the soil deeper, permitting the roots to go deeper as well. This promotes healthier turf. In actual practice, most parklands do not receive any extra watering, and the grass is not harmed even if it turns brown and goes into a dormant state. Athletic fields and the parks in business districts may need extra watering. To strike a compromise between lush green lawns and dry brown lawns while still conserving water, begin watering only when the grass develops a slight purplish color.

Insect and Disease Control

In many parks of below-average attendance, insect and disease control do not require any special treatment other than careful observation and spot treatment as necessary. Healthy turf and controlled cultural practices will prevent most invasions except the isolated problems here and there that most park managers can live with. Chapter 20 will provide additional information on pest management.

Turf Renovation

The figures described in this paragraph illustrate how an athletic field's turf can be efficiently renovated. Figure 14.2 shows the field before any work is done. Figure

Fig. 14.2

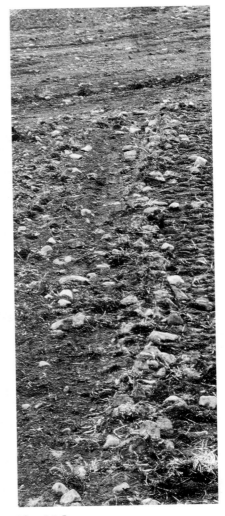

Fig. 14.3

14.3 shows the field after rototilling to eliminate the weeds and aerate the soil. Figure 14.4 illustrates the same field after the rocks and debris are removed. The next step (Fig. 14.5) involves raking and leveling the field so the rocks and debris can be picked up (Fig. 14.6). Fertilizer, lime, and seed are then applied as necessary (Fig. 14.7), and the field is raked again. New seedlings can be seen in Fig. 14.8 and established turf in Fig. 14.9.

Wear Tolerance

Wear on athletic fields causes major safety problems while wear in parks becomes an aesthetic problem. Wear injury is a result of foot and vehicular traffic crushing the grass plants and compacting the soil so the grass dies. Wear is corrected through

Fig. 14.4

Fig. 14.5

Fig. 14.6

Fig. 14.7

a major program to improve the soil by relieving compaction and by the use of wear-tolerant grasses. Adding sand to a heavy soil will improve drainage, which in turn prevents soil compaction from games played after rainstorms. Perennial ryegrass, tall fescue, and other grasses described in the grass summary (Fig. 23.12 on page 202) in Chap. 23, produce fibrous cell walls that resist wear on the plant crown. Wear tolerance can also be improved through higher mowing heights, irrigation, and proper fertilization. Higher-than-normal levels of potassium will also enhance wear tolerance. The recuperative potential of such grasses as Kentucky bluegrass is also important by indicating the recovery rate after excessive wear has occurred. Fast-growing bluegrass rhizomes recover faster than ryegrass clumps. Yet a blend of bluegrass and ryegrass produces superior wear tolerance from the

Fig. 14.8

Fig. 14.9

ryegrass and excellent recovery from the bluegrass. Certain cultivars of grasses are also wear-tolerant and should be used in high wear areas. The cultivars suitable for wear tolerance change every few years as better cultivars replace older ones. In the mid-1990s, good wear-tolerant bluegrass cultivars included A-34, Glade, Sydsport, Trenton, and Wabash; perennial ryegrasses included Diplomat, Gator, Ovation, Prelude, and SR4000; and tall fescues included Jaguar, Mesa, Rebel, Rebel II, and Tribute. Wear tolerance is also improved if traffic is spread out over a larger area. Practice fields and game fields should be different. Similar events should not be scheduled on the same field, and traffic patterns should be changed frequently. In a park environment with crowding problems, consider rounding walk intersections, making the walk wider, using stepping stones in bare spots, and developing plans

Fig. 14.10

that highlight the problem locations. Just observing the park's use patterns will often provide the solution to wear problems.

The Final Touch

The turf maintenance program should include a program that does not affect the turf grass but does promote the recognition that maintenance is being performed. The final touch consists of tree, shrub, and flower planting. Flowers (see Fig. 14.10) are especially effective at drawing attention to maintenance efforts. The planting does not have to be a major one, just enough to capture the attention of the park user. Consider something as simple as a naturalized planting of daffodils surrounding several tree trunks. The placement of picnic tables or benches nearby will allow for a full appreciation of the site. Such touches compliment and draw attention to the efforts made on the fields. All of these recommendations can be followed whether you care for your lawn yourself or pay a landscape contractor to do it for you.

References

Gaussoin, Roch E., "Choosing Traffic–Tolerant Turfgrass Varieties," *Sports Turf*, July 1994: 25–26.

Hall, John R., III, "Buying Sod," *Grounds Maintenance*, August 1994: 14–16.

Hall, Ron, "Turf Pros Respond to Biostimulants," *Landscape Management*, October 1994: 8.

Town of Wellesley, Park and Tree Division, Wellesley, Massachusetts, "Lawn Care" (information bulletin), 1985.

Mowing

Mowing is stressful to grass. Stress causes the grass plant to stop functioning. Water is lost from the cut blades, and the roots have to stop growing in order to absorb water. To minimize this stress, the turf should be mowed as often as necessary to remove no more than one third the leaf blade length and leave the grass 2 to 2½ inches in height during the spring season. The turf is cut at 3 inches during the summer and winter months to increase drought and extreme temperature tolerance. During the fall, the height can be lowered again until Thanksgiving. The direction of cut can also change according to the amount of field play and the season. Mowing below the recommended height or too much at one time will weaken the grass and increase disease problems. The higher cut will also provide the grass clippings with a place to "hide" until they decompose. Studies have also reported that grass at 2½ to 3 inches will actually grow more slowly than at a lower height. This will increase the time interval between mowings.

Mowers

Mowing can be done with three types of mowers: reel, rotary, or flail. Reel mowers are very effective at low cutting heights (see Fig. 15.1) and are excellent for golf courses. They give a high-quality appearance. However, they are not good for tall grass, weeds, uneven ground, rocks and sticks, and mower maintenance. Rotary mowers, which cut the grass by slicing it horizontally, (see Fig. 15.2) are better able to handle tall grass and weeds and are very good for park work. Sharp blades are necessary for a clean cut. Rotary mowers are much easier to maintain and are better suited to mulching applications and/or the bagging of clippings. They do not

Fig. 15.1

suffer as much damage when the blades hit rocks and debris. Flail mowers (see Fig. 15.3) are a combination of the reel and rotary types. The flail shaft is horizontal like the reel, but the blades are small knives that cut the grass like a rotary. The knives are on hinges or chain links so the knife will fall back if a rock or debris is hit, making the mower much safer. Flail mowers are excellent for mulching grass and leaves and for use in parks and infrequently mowed areas. Incidentally, reverse rotating flails give a very high quality cut.

Fig. 15.2

Fig. 15.3

The Jacobson HR-15 gang mower, the three-mower Interstater system, the 16-foot Toro 580D, and comparable mowers make 15- or 16-foot-wide cuts using high-quality rotary blades that mow large areas quite fast and at the same time cut off seed heads in the summer months. All of this ultimately produces a better-looking result than do reel mowers. These mowers easily handle the tall grass during the spring growth surge so the raking of grass clippings and clumps is greatly reduced. They also cut wet grass so the mowing will not fall behind schedule on damp days. Trimming should follow the large mower within a day or two. Consider purchasing riding mowers with 60- or 72-inch decks that will cut grass while mowing at 7 mph, twice the speed of 48- or 52-inch walk-behinds. In addition to the increase in speed, these mowers can be driven on the sidewalks from park to park in some situations, so time is saved by avoiding loading and unloading at every single park.

Grass is inexpensive to plant but very expensive to maintain. Other plants cost more to purchase but require less care. The biggest maintenance problem and budget item is usually the mowing of grass. While the most obvious shortcut might be increasing the size of the mower width, a maintenance map will determine what size and type of mower is best suited for each area of parkland. The largest mower should be used first, and the operator should mow as close to edges and obstructions as possible, without losing speed or mowing efficiency. The trimming is then done with smaller mowers set at the same mowing height. Ideally, the lawn areas should be designed with curves within the turning capability of the largest mower used in each area. By keeping the mowers moving continuously and with a minimum number of sharp corners, obstruction trimming or repeat mowing can be reduced significantly. When the grass needs to be raked, a lawn sweeper should be used to pick up the clumps. Another technique for solving the grass clippings problem involves mowing the area again three days after the clumps first appear.

Never waste taxpayers' money raking by hand unless absolutely necessary. Under normal circumstances, when rotary mowers are used the mowing should begin along the outside edge and circle toward the center of the area being mowed. Be sure the grass is tossed toward the center so that if the grass needs sweeping, only the center of the area rather than the entire area will need to be picked up. Blowing the grass clippings into the center also recuts many of the blades so they will fall into the grass and become invisible.

Design

Mowing around obstructions such as posts and poles, hydrants, signs, and fences is the most time-wasting feature of any park mowing project. If removal is impossible, relocating or combining obstructions should perhaps be considered as an option. You may also want to consider the construction of a permanent mow strip next to the obstruction so at least the trimming is eliminated. Another way to solve this problem involves combining all the obstructions into one large shrub or flower bed. Keep in mind the impact any changes might have in terms of transferred maintenance. For example, if creating islands around two obstructions closes the distance between them such that the mower will not fit through it, don't do it! Similarly, if the shrub beds created result in more maintenance than mowing around the obstruction, don't do it! Beds can be enhanced with shrubs, flowers, ornamental grasses, and occasionally large rocks or earth mounds that beautify the area. Flower and shrub beds can also make attractive substitutions for lawns and fences while promoting a recognition of the landscape's design and maintenance. It is also easier and cheaper to pull weeds than to mow grass for 20 weeks.

Also consider annual or semiannual mowing only in natural or low-visibility areas. Hay rights can also be sold in certain situations. Minimizing complaints about creating "meadows" or "prairies" can be accomplished by either screening the area from public view or delineating the meadow with a mowed edge. This gives the impression that the meadow is deliberate, and the mowed edge lets residents know that although the maintenance policy has been modified the area is still being taken care of.

Mulching Mowers

The use of mulching mowers should be standard everywhere. These mowers have special decks that suspend the clippings in the air so they can be rechopped by special blades. Mulching blades must be kept sharp and the motor run at a high speed. This process of chopping grass clippings repeatedly and leaving them in the turf is also called "grasscycling." A lawn will be healthier because the grass clippings will decompose and the nutrients will be absorbed by the grass root system within 14 days. Mulching does not build up thatch but it does reduce fertilizer requirements by as much as 30 percent. On an annual basis, grass mulching will return to the soil 6 pounds of nitrogen, 1 pound of phosphorus, and 4 pounds of potassium per 1000 square feet. Because the grass clippings are about 85 percent water, a 25 percent reduction in watering requirements can be expected through grasscycling. The clippings also add organic matter to the soil that increases water penetration into the soil. Grass clippings also shade the soil and prevent water from evaporating. If discharge decks are used, the clippings should be blown into the area not yet mowed so the clippings will be rechopped smaller. Grasscycling is better for the lawn as well as for the environment.

Trimming and Edging

Trimmer mowing is reduced by using mulched shrub beds and by riding with one wheel of the mower deck on the mulch (as seen in Fig. 15.1). Use mulch around all the trees in highly visible parks (see Fig. 11.7 on page 114). The mulch needs frequent replacement to keep weeds under control and to keep mowers and trimmers from damaging the tree trunks. The use of Surflan, the preemergent weed killer, is far better than weed whips operated by temporary or inexperienced laborers. To eliminate trimming, high curbs or low walls may be substituted for railings and fences, provided the top of the curb is set flush with the surface to be mowed. The rear discharge mower will eliminate damage next to trees as well as grass clippings in the streets or the shrub beds.

Steep Banks

Steep banks (greater than 3:1) offer some very difficult maintenance situations. Water runoff will also be higher in these areas. Common solutions to consider include building a wall and leveling off the top and bottom of the steep bank; covering the slope with ground cover and mulch to eliminate frequent and expensive mowing; allowing the bank to become naturalized with native plants, meadow grasses, tree seedlings, and the like; and if all else fails, paving the slope (but don't forget to consider drainage changes that will result from this action).

Shade

Shade makes growing grass very difficult. Luckily, many blends of seed mix are available for growing grasses that tolerate shade. However, shade during more than 60 percent of the day makes it almost impossible for any grass to grow. Grass will grow in shade if there are unlimited funds and resources for labor and fertilizer. Some alternatives include a planting of annual ryegrass or bluegrass every year in the early spring; a planting of a shade-loving ground cover such as pachysandra, wild ginger, vinca, English or Boston ivy, or euonymous; naturalizing the site with shrubs, mulch, and forest leaves; thinning the trees and raising the branches; cutting the grass only a ½-inch higher than the grass in the sun; and heavily mulching the site to eliminate all growth.

Extra care should be given during the period when the leaves are off the trees and the grass is growing. Keep leaves off the grass so they will not mat and smother it.

Weeding

Between 2 and 4 inches of mulch should be applied to control weeds in shrub beds. Mulch is a great labor-saving device, not to mention its water conservation and long-term soil improvement properties. Surflan and Roundup are used in most areas for complete long-term weed control. Because herbicides cannot be used everywhere, fabric or sheets of newspaper covered with mulch solve these weed problems. The mulch will need to be inspected frequently to keep the fabric covered.

References

Ingham, Daniel, "Grasscycling Back into the Future," *Landscape and Irrigation*, April 1994: 8–10.

————, "Reel vs. Rotary Mowers," *Landscape and Irrigation*, January 1994: 18–19.

16
Ball Field Management

Design

Baseball fields should always look good, but more importantly they should always be safe. Safety requires that the turf be weed-free and the surface be level and free of stones, sticks, and anything else in the soil. Ball fields must be properly built and properly managed. Since the athlete is there to play a game, his or her attention is focused on the game and not the field. The fields are often in continuous use throughout the entire growing season, so field maintenance becomes even more difficult. The turf manager, therefore, must be a professional, who is knowledgeable about and up to date on the latest techniques in field maintenance.

Selecting a grass for the field will require study to determine which variety, cultivar, or blend is most suitable for the field. Consideration should be given to wear tolerance, soil, climate, cutting height, resiliency, and uniformity. The infield area will come in different sizes, depending on the game—baseball, softball, little league, and so on. The skinned area includes the base paths, home plate area, and pitcher's mound and sometimes the dugout runways and warning tracks. Sometimes softball and little leagues have no grass in the infield, and the entire area is maintained with clay, a fine stone dust, river bottom silt, sand, or fine crushed brick. Sometimes mixes with clay are also available. The brick, which is commonly used on the West Coast, may look good, but it wears out the baseballs, uniforms, and footwear quite quickly.

Renovation versus Reconstruction

Ballfields are rebuilt in two ways: renovation—that is, a field replacement project— and reconstruction—a total field, backstop, and base pads replacement project.

Renovations are low cost and will usually pay for themselves within a year, while reconstruction might take five years to repay. The cost savings come from reduced turf care, quick and easy infield maintenance, and other innovations stemming from field renovation.

Drainage is a necessity. If a drainage system exists on a field, it must be kept operational. If a new one is required, it should be built like a French drain, wherein gravel is laid over the trenches where a drainpipe has been installed. The gravel should fill the trench except for the top 3 inches. The top layer should consist of a sand/topsoil mix and grass seed or sod. The trenches should be parallel and about 30 feet apart. On a baseball field, a trench should ring the perimeter of the infield area and the outfield as necessary. The French drain concept works quite well, but it does require renovation every five years or so.

Clay migration on the infield causes a ridge to form between the infield and the turf. This prevents the water from escaping the infield, and it must be removed before a game. Compacted soil stays wet for days and must be modified or replaced to a depth of 2 to 4 inches. When being rebuilt, ball fields' skinned areas should be excavated to subsoil and the clay added in layers. Each layer should be leveled and compacted until it meets the final grade. The final layer is simply added to the surface and raked level. It should not be rolled. The result is a safe, easily maintained surface.

Management

The infield will need the most maintenance. After every storm, the rainwater needs to be removed before any game can be played. Do not push the water off the clay and into the grass because the clay then builds up in the grass, shortening the life of the field. It is better to make a hole in the center of a puddle and lift the water out with a hand pump or an empty can. The water should be dumped into a pail and taken away from the field. When the puddles are gone, the field can be dried out with fresh clay or calcined clay drying products such as Turface or Speedy Dry.

The grass on the infield needs to be mowed just before the game to ensure uniformity and fast play. The clay needs to be leveled and powder lines laid down before each game as well. When leveling or raking the field, pull the clay from the edge and raise the center of the skinned areas. The pitcher's mound and home plate areas can often have large holes from excessive use by the end of each game. These holes must be filled in before the next game by adding more clay and firmly tamping it in place. After dragging and preparing the infield, the grass should be swept with a broom to move the clay back into the skinned area. Finally, the clay should be watered prior to each game to reduce holes, wear and tear, and dust kicked up during the game. Weeds and grass should be removed from the edge of the skinned area annually with a sod cutter, edger, or herbicide. On heavily used fields, fertilization should be done every four weeks. The type of fertilizer used should be based on the results of a soil test, and it can be applied as recommended in Chap. 14 on turf management.

All of these maintenance steps require tight scheduling and communication so the groundskeeper can have the fields prepared for the game and maintenance can be performed between games. Maintenance is essential to providing a safe playing surface and ensuring low liability for the landowner.

Field Marking

Marking the white lines around home plate is something of an art. The lines on a baseball infield are usually made with gypsum powder, which is applied with a push spreader. The groundskeeper should first level and smooth the entire infield (see Fig. 16.1). The base lines are painted by following a string (see Fig. 16.2). The lines in the home plate area are best laid down by using a jig as a guide. Jigs can be purchased from a ball field supply house or made by the groundskeeper (see Figs. 16.3 and 16.4). This does away with the need to calculate and measure the lines for every game. After the lines are laid on the infield (see Fig. 16.5), it is raked again (see Figs. 16.6 and 16.7).

White latex paint is used for the lines in the field's grass areas (see Fig. 16.8). By mixing a plant growth retardant or herbicide into the athletic field marking paint, the painted grass won't grow and the paint consequently won't get mowed off. The amount of herbicide or growth retardant used is determined by using the diluted paint as the liquid required for the herbicide dilution. This decreases the painting frequency, the amount of paint required, and the time required to do the field layout and painting. If herbicide is used, the lines will need to be reseeded at the end of the season. The paint should be cheap and diluted two or three times so it flows smoothly through the paint machine yet thick enough to create a bright line that lasts several weeks. Softball and little

Fig. 16.1

league fields should have skinned infields wherever possible. A simple drag and laborers with rakes can easily groom the infield.

Renovations

Every year the field will need to be leveled. This is especially critical around the base pads where the clay has moved into or under the turf and the area has been raised up. The easiest way to do this is to cut away the sod, level the soil and infield clay, and resod the area. The field's large grass areas should be leveled by topdressing. Soil modifications can be done the same way. If the soil has become heavy and compact, repeated topdressings of sand will gradually loosen the soil. If the soil needs organic material, compost should be added. One technique that works well in the northern parts of the United States, where major top-

Fig. 16.2

dressing applications are necessary, is to wait until the ground is frozen and send a highway sander over the turf with clean sand, compost, or other materials. The sander can be calibrated to the desired depth of application. The materials being

Fig. 16.3

Fig. 16.4

Fig. 16.5

Fig. 16.6

Fig. 16.7

Fig. 16.8

spread, however, have to be delivered to the park daily so they do not freeze into lumps. After spring thaws and rains the materials will be washed in, and spring sports activities will take care of mixing the material into the topsoil.

References

Kurtz, Kent W., "Baseball Field Maintenance," *Park Maintenance*, March 1979: 22–27.

Portz, H. L., "Baseball Field Renovation," *Weeds, Trees and Turf*, June 1983: 28 ff.

17 Pruning

Trees and shrubs are pruned to preserve their health and appearance while keeping them safe for people and property. Pruning also enhances the structural integrity, longevity, and functional value of plants in the urban environment. Plants must also be pruned to remove dead, damaged, and dangerous branches. Pruning can be performed at any time of the year except at bud break. The timing of pruning—for example, immediately after flowering and never during heavy sap flow—is also critical to certain species. Plants that flower on new wood can be pruned any time a flush of new growth is desired. Deciduous plants can be pruned when dormant, and fall flower or fruiting plants can be pruned in late winter. Evergreens can be pruned any time the new growth is not soft. Pruning should only be performed by workers who have been trained in proper pruning techniques. To the untrained eye, a tree or shrub may appear to be in good condition, but the trained pruner with years of experience can spot problems and defects long before a problem occurs.

Pruning Young Trees

Young trees should be pruned to ensure a straight, strong trunk; one central leader; high branches; and a well-balanced crown. Pruning newly planted trees involves "training" them to develop proper shapes, to remove narrow-angled branches with included bark, to correct poorly attached branches, to develop structural strength, to remove any dead or damaged branches, and to ensure low maintenance at maturity. Three years and seven years after planting, young trees should be pruned again to remove any dead, damaged, diseased, or objectional branches.

Once a routine pruning cycle is established and a couple of cycles have been completed certain trees will reach a point at which pruning is not necessary. The cycle should be continued, however, because all trees can benefit from the inspection that accompanies pruning whether pruning is done or not, and other trees will always need pruning. Because systematic pruning improves tree health, integrated pest management programs (see Chap. 20) are less necessary, there is less potential for damage claims against the city, and because the trees live longer removal costs are deferred. A tree climber and aerial lift can handle the pruning of 500 park trees a year on a routine schedule.

Pruning Shrubs

Many parks have overgrown shrubs that they would like to prune back to a reasonable size. Pruning should be done to preserve the health and appearance of the plant while at the same time enhancing its structural integrity, longevity, and value. The best time to prune is right after flowering. When pruning any plant, you should first remove dead, diseased, or damaged branches before trimming the remaining branches to reduce the size of the plant. Pruning young branches guides the growth in the direction of the buds and also encourages vigor in the remaining branches. Small wounds also heal fast and are less detrimental to a plant. Making the same cuts many years later results in wounds that can cause major stress to the plant. Although not always possible, the best time to prune is when the plants are dormant.

All cuts should be made as close to the trunk or parent limb as possible without cutting into the branch collar or leaving a protruding stub (see Figs. 17.1 to 17.5 below). When shortening a branch, make sure the lateral branch is at least half the diameter of the branch being removed so weak sprouts are not forced to grow. Treating cuts with wound dressing is not recommended. Sharp tools that make clean cuts should be used at all times.

Fig. 17.1   **Fig. 17.2**   **Fig. 17.3**   **Fig. 17.4**   **Fig. 17.5**

Reducing the size of a shrub can seem much more difficult than it actually is. First inspect the shrub, and carefully select each branch to be removed. Always cut back to a branch crotch, and be sure to make each cut carefully. If all this fails to meet your expectations, cut the largest stems down to 12 inches from the ground and wait. The stump should send out new branches, and within two years the shrub will have sprouted and again be ready for pruning. An alternative technique that also works very well is to remove one-third of the shrub's main trunks every year for three years. By leaving a 6-to-12-inch stump, you will enable most shrubs to resprout with new growth. After three years, the entire shrub is rejuvenated.

Many park managers would like more flowers to appear. Most shrubs can easily be encouraged to set flower buds if the old flower stalks are taken off the shrub soon after flowering. This is accomplished by snapping the flower stalk to the side. Be careful to break off all the seed pods, but do not go so far down the stalk that desirable young leaves and buds are broken off.

Pruning Techniques

The methods used for pruning and branch removal will vary depending upon the size, species, and function of the plant. Pruning trees and shrubs is best done using the following guidelines.

A. As mentioned, all cuts should be made as close as possible to the trunk or parent limb without cutting into the branch collar or leaving a protruding stub (as illustrated in Fig. 17.1). When cutting small branches at the bud, you should avoid a steep angle of cut (as shown in Fig. 17.2), a cut too far from the bud (as shown in Fig. 17.3), or a cut too close to the bud (as shown in Fig. 17.4). Figure 17.5 is just right.

B. All branches too large to support with one hand should be precut to avoid splitting or tearing of the bark. Precutting involves removing the branch safely by first undercutting (see Fig. 17.6) and then overcutting 3 or 4 inches from the crotch (see Fig. 17.7). The stub (see Fig. 17.8) is removed with the third cut. When shortening a lateral branch, it should be at least half the diameter of the branch being removed so sprouts are not encouraged to grow.

C. Treatment of cuts with wound dressing is not recommended but may be used for cosmetic purposes.

D. Old injuries, cables, and so on should be inspected on an annual basis.

E. Sharp tools that make clean cuts should be used at all times.

F. All cut limbs should be removed from the tree. Small branches can be thrown down, but larger branches must be lowered with ropes.

G. Pruning should be timed to avoid insect or disease infestation.

H. Remove the weaker or less desirable of two crossed branches.

I. Pruning more than one-third the plant's total leaf area will encourage weak sucker growth.

Fig. 17.6

Fig. 17.7

Fig. 17.8

When branches are properly removed, the callus will grow equally around the entire cut, forming a ring or donut. The proper cut at the collar heals much faster than the flush cut. Climbing irons should not be used on live trees except for tree removal or emergency rescue. Keep in mind that whenever a gaffe enters the tree or a branch is cut, the tree is injured. This leads to decay causing microorganisms, diseases, and insects to enter the tree before it can "compartmentalize" them and grow a callus to cover the wound.

Root Pruning

If roots become exposed and damaged during transplanting, storms, or construction, they should be pruned. The pruning techniques for roots are identical to those for pruning branches. The cuts should be clean, smooth, and at a crotch.

Tree Removal

Most parks and cities can plan through natural attrition to remove approximately 1 to 2 percent of their tree population every year. A 1 percent removal rate reflects a 100-year life cycle, and 2 percent indicates a 50-year cycle. Trees have to be removed because of death; hazardous conditions; "untreelike" conditions in old, severely pruned trees; and undesirability due to species, fruiting habits, or pest problems. Because trees can become an emotional issue, the public needs to be educated about the need for tree removal. Removing trees before they are actually dead, for example, can cause negative public reactions. In our urban society, harvesting trees is generally unacceptable. This gives park managers no choice but to leave old trees on their own and prune for safety. When the tree has declined 90 percent, most people will let it go.

References

Boerner, Deborah A., "Nurturing New Trees," *Urban Forests*, June/July 1990: 9.

Miller, Dr. Robert W., *Urban Forestry, Planning and Managing Urban Greenspaces*, Englewood Cliffs, NJ: Prentice Hall, 1988.

National Arborist Association, *Pruning Standards for Shade Trees*, New Hampshire: National Arborist Association, 1988.

Shigo, Alex L., *A New Tree Biology*, Shigo and Trees, 1989.

18

Management Staff

People are the key components of any successful park system. Although most of this book has discussed people involved with the planning phase of park success, this chapter deals with the unsung heroes of the successful park—the management and maintenance staff. Organizing the staff into a smooth-running operation is key to this success.

Maintenance Zones

All maintenance work throughout the grounds maintenance system should be carefully planned and evaluated. During this process, the workload should be divided up into maintenance zones. Assign employees, vehicles, and tools to these zones for the entire season. Let the groundskeeper in charge determine work assignments within the guidelines prepared by the field supervisor. Pride in a maintenance zone means a thorough knowledge of the zone's needs and labor requirements and results in fewer repairs to equipment. This is a great morale and productivity booster. The crew knows what has to be done and when it has to be done, and it has the resources to do it as efficiently as possible. For example, trash barrels are emptied as needed based on the groundskeeper's experience rather than every barrel, every day.

As many employees as possible should be assigned to field stations in their zones where time clocks, tools, and vehicles are stored. This will eliminate daily trips back and forth to the central garage, and it will allow the worker to start the day by walking into the park instead of waiting for a daily assignment and then driving to the site.

An Example

One example of a maintenance zone that has worked successfully is Wellesley, Massachusetts.

All park and public lands maintained by the Wellesley Park and Tree Division are included in one of nine separate maintenance zones. Figure 18.1 shows a map of Wellesley's open space and the zone assignments. Daily maintenance assignments in each zone are determined by the superintendent based on needs, weather, and availability of personnel and equipment. The groundskeeper in charge of a zone implements assignments according to the following priorities: mowing followed by emptying trash barrels, vandalism repairs, seasonal requirements such as field lining, special projects and capital improvements, mulching, and finally tree and shrub trimming, which is usually reserved for the winter months.

This program has been in effect since 1977, and from the beginning the employees have been enthusiastic about their maintenance zones. Each groundskeeper has developed pride in his or her zone and knows it thoroughly. This has resulted in increased efficiency through knowing what has to be done, when, and how. The system has worked so well that the budget system has been changed from a work activity accounting system to actual costs per zone.

Each groundskeeper is permanently assigned to a small dump truck, flatbed, or other piece of equipment for the entire season. This is intended to reduce down-

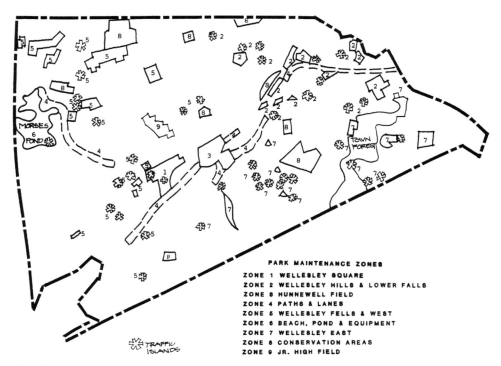

PARK MAINTENANCE ZONES
ZONE 1 WELLESLEY SQUARE
ZONE 2 WELLESLEY HILLS & LOWER FALLS
ZONE 3 HUNNEWELL FIELD
ZONE 4 PATHS & LANES
ZONE 5 WELLESLEY FELLS & WEST
ZONE 6 BEACH, POND & EQUIPMENT
ZONE 7 WELLESLEY EAST
ZONE 8 CONSERVATION AREAS
ZONE 9 JR. HIGH FIELD

Fig. 18.1

time and increase productivity. Tool boxes on the trucks eliminate the need for extra trips back to the garage for forgotten tools and for making routine repairs. The crew goes from park to park on an assigned route. Many small parks are mowed by a two-person crew with a truck, which tows a trailer containing two mowers and a trimmer.

The zone system, taken collectively, has resulted in no additional employees despite the addition of 125 acres of passive recreation-conservation land transferred to the division for routine maintenance. For one year only, an additional employee was needed to assist in the care of an additional 90 acres of active recreation land when all school grounds maintenance was transferred to the Park and Tree Division. All but one school was absorbed into the zone system, and that school was put into a new zone with this additional employee in charge.

Zone maintenance for this department has greatly reduced labor needs while increasing productivity and improving employee morale.

Maintenance Costs

Look at maintenance costs on a per-acre basis to locate areas where costs might be unusually high. Each park and each maintenance zone should be accountable. To provide some guidance, Fig. 18.2 describes how three cities compare with each other in 1990 dollars per acre. Dallas, Texas, a large city in the dry South, has a $46 million budget and 490 employees; Wellesley, Massachusetts, in wet New England, has a $700,000 budget and 19 employees; and Westerville, Ohio, located outside Columbus, has 32,500 residents, a budget of $523,000, and 9 employees.

Fig. 18.2 Costs

Park Type	Dallas	Wellesley	Westerville
1. Conservation area: Very low maintenance, annual mowing, regular litter pickup, periodic inspection (cost per acre).	$ 800	$ 100	$ 20
2. Parks without irrigation, frequent mowing, regular litter pickup (cost per acre).	5,600	400	28
3. High-quality turf, irrigation, weekly mowing (cost per acre).	7,000	1,000	40
4. Same as park #3 plus seasonal flowers (cost per acre).	10,000	2,500	125
5. Class A ball diamond (cost per field).	10,000	4,000	35
6. Trail inspection, cleanup, signs (cost per mile).	2,000	1,300	140
7. Irrigation (cost per acre).	2,500	200	—
8. Traffic island maintenance with landscaping instead of pavement (cost per acre).	—	1,671	98
9. Litter pickup (cost per week, per acre).	—	2	4
10. Total tree maintenance (cost per tree).	—	9	38

When true costs are known, efforts can be focused on ways to reduce the high cost generators. For example, in Wellesley, traffic islands in one maintenance zone were costing approximately $7000 per acre annually. Five years later after a major traffic island improvement program, the costs were down to $1700 per acre, which was much closer to the citywide average.

Municipal Staff versus Contractors

Which is less expensive, using a contractor; paying by the job plus profit; or maintaining municipal staff paid year-round plus benefits? Most city managers often ask this question as they search for ways to provide the required municipal services for the lowest possible cost. Park maintenance services can be provided by using contractors, in-house staff, or combinations of both.

The advantages of in-house crews include having people available to do anything and everything that needs to be done while meeting the community's quality standards. The community also has an identity or personality that is reflected in the maintenance of its parks. Quality control is better with in-house crews because they must live with their mistakes and be proud of their accomplishments. In-house crews can be kept busy year-round with all phases of park maintenance. The crews are able to respond to emergencies quickly, and the workforce is generally more stable. No administrative time is needed to write and oversee contracts. This provides some variety to the daily routine, making the job more enjoyable for the park worker. In-house crews can also become specialized and just as productive as contracted labor. In most situations, deciding among contracting, in-house staff, or a combination of both is usually made on the basis of cost, quality of service desired, and past practice.

Typical contracted services include planting, pruning, turf care, flower growing and maintenance, general maintenance, trash removal, and management consulting for writing and overseeing contracts, preparing all types of documents, and conforming to all regulations.

Some examples of the advantages of contracted park work include the following:

1. Costs are lower (depending on how costs are calculated).
2. Labor is available for peak work periods or overload requirements.
3. Cancellation can be made by phone when work is not available or the weather is poor.
4. Contractor provides employees with supervision and training.
5. Contractors are specialists, which makes them more efficient.
6. There is no pay for work that does not meet specified quality standards.
7. The city can easily switch to in-house staff if it wants a change.
8. Contractors are motivated by profit.
9. Infrequently used or specialized services can be obtained at a reasonable cost.
10. Quality can be obtained with well-written contracts.

Regardless of whether the work is done by park employees or by contracted labor, it is important that everyone takes pride in his or her work. When a project is done, it should look nice and meet the standards required by the city. While workers may not be interested in doing projects that will not be seen by the public or seem very insignificant, they need to know the project will make future maintenance easier or more efficient or that there is some other reason for doing it. Workers should know the maintenance level that is acceptable. Are there cleanliness standards? Are there standards for mowing, pruning, mulching, weeding, and the like? Let the grounds crew know what is acceptable so it can develop respect for itself and pride in its performance. Review its performance occasionally and ask for suggestions for making the job easier or better and in any event more productive.

Contract Preparation

Assuming that a city has carefully evaluated in-house versus contract services and that the decision has been made to have all or some services provided by contract, it might be advisable to obtain the services of a consultant to prepare the contract documents. There are three types of contracts available. They are a unit price contract in which the work is bid on a unit item, a lump sum contract that requires one price for the whole job, and a time and materials contract that requires the bidder to specify hourly rates for workers and equipment plus a percentage above costs for materials. These costs are billed to the city on a regular basis for actual work done.

The contract document contains a certain number of requirements. The first item is a bid advertisement that is prepared for the local newspaper's legal notices section. It becomes a part of the contract documents. This advertisement should indicate what is being bid on, when and where the bid is to be opened, a reference number for the contract, the name of the department requesting the bid, and any other items the state's or municipality's attorney may require. The next part of the contract is the body, and it contains an introduction, general provisions, specific conditions, and a conclusion. This section is followed by the bid sheet. It is here that the items being bid on are summarized, and a bidder can indicate his or her bid price in written and numerical form. The final part of the bid contains the signatures, corporate requirements, minimum wage rates, and other legal requirements dictated by state and local regulations, ordinances, or bylaws.

Contracts need to be written so they are fair, they are accurate, and they reflect good supervision. Contractors will often loan a set of specifications to the municipality that reflects their preferences and the specifications that have been made by others. Contracts need to be written in more or less quantities. If the contract is being written to provide a service, for example, it can provide for 24-hour emergency service, requiring the contractor to be on site within 2 hours of notification.

Before making an award, ask the potential contractor for references, names of other clients, and a list of completed projects. Contact references, and interview the contractors at their job sites. Find out what people like and don't like about the contractor. Look at the contractor's employees and equipment. Are they suitable for working in your municipality?

When new contractors are awarded work, they should be given your mainte-nance standards for reference as well as maps for locating their sites. The contrac-tor provides a supervisor who reports on location with the crew. The contractor is also given handouts so he or she can answer common questions and explain the services being provided. Contractors do not, however, speak for the city.

People

Managing employees can be difficult at times. The consequences of alcoholism and drug abuse in the workplace are realized in lower productivity, increased absenteeism, inefficiency, increased turnover, increased injury rates, and incidents arising from behavioral problems. Employees with these problems can be disrup-tive and demoralizing to others, and this leads to excessive turnover and low morale.

Employee Assistance Programs

Many municipalities believe that employees with problems require professional assistance. Early detection of these conditions by the employer is essential for an effective program of evaluation, treatment, and rehabilitation. Concern with alco-holism and drug abuse is a basic management responsibility. Supervisors are expected to be familiar with their employees' appearance, behavior, and work pat-terns and to be on the alert for any changes. These could result from other causes such as illness, prescribed drugs, and fatigue. Supervisors should help employees seek medical help if necessary.

Once a supervisor has determined that an employee needs professional assis-tance, he or she should contact the personnel department or a community agency that specializes in the cure of drug or alcohol dependency. When planning to deal with drug or alcohol abuse, a municipality must also establish a written policy that conforms to the law. This policy must be carefully prepared and be made known to all employees in the same manner as a safety policy. Employee-assistance pro-grams are implemented by enlightened management to help employees deal with alcohol and other behavioral problems that interfere with job performance. Pro-grams of this type enable a department to retain valued employees.

Labor Unions

Another employee asset that management has to deal with in many communities is the labor union. Management should carefully consider the value unions have and how it can exploit labor negotiations to its advantage. Management should negotiate for contracts that provide room to manage in exchange for employee raises and benefits. For example, offer flextime in exchange for hikes in the longevity bonus, and so on.

Inspect union contracts carefully so you understand exactly what can and can-not be done. Stretch the "cans" creatively by gradually establishing a past practice or by exercising management rights that are implied but not clearly stated. Don't be afraid of a grievance if a point can be made or management can gain substantially even if it loses the specific issue.

Also be sure to be flexible in all actions. For example, during employee disciplinary actions make the first suspension for two days so if there is a need to compromise you can drop back to one day and the point will still have been made. During disciplinary actions use a progressive policy (first abuse—two days, second abuse—one week, third abuse—one month, and fourth abuse—termination), and document everything!

Sick Leave Abuse

Like many communities faced with problems of sick leave abuse, the Wellesley Department of Public Works instituted a two-phase attack on absenteeism in the 1970s that has proved itself to be successful. The first approach began in 1978 during the union contract negotiation process. At that time, an incentive program was proposed in which employees were granted leave with pay for personal days as a bonus for not taking sick time. One personal leave day was granted at the end of every quarter if no sick days were taken during that quarter. Employees who had not used more than five total sick days during the previous year were also entitled to a bonus of one additional personal business day.

This personal day program resulted in a very positive attitude among the department's employees and improved morale considerably. However, because the bonus system still did not provide sufficient incentive for the 5 or 10 percent of the workforce who continued to abuse sick leave, in 1981 the department undertook the development of a uniform policy for administering tardiness and sick leave. This policy stated that after four days of sick leave in a given year the employee should be issued a notice, and progressive discipline should increase with continued sick leave abuse. If after five days of absence without pay the supervisor determines that sick leave abuse has occurred, the employee is subject to additional disciplinary action up to and including discharge. The policy also provides detailed definitions of tardiness, absenteeism, and methods for determining tardiness and sick leave abuse.

These rules are implemented uniformly in all divisions within the department. Despite disciplinary actions and discharges made in accordance with these rules, the union has not challenged the rules at any arbitration hearings.

As Fig. 18.3 illustrates, both programs have had remarkable results. For example, in 1977 the Highway Division averaged 10 days of absence per employee during the year. Since then, however, that figure has decreased every year to the 1982 average of four days of absence per employee per year. In addition, in 1983 almost half of the 25 employees in the Park and Tree Division had perfect attendance. Another measure of the improved performance was reflected in the fact that this division lost 29 workdays due to sickness in 1993, while other employees earned 32 personal days for good attendance. By comparison, over 200 workdays due to illness were lost per year before these programs went into effect. This dramatic

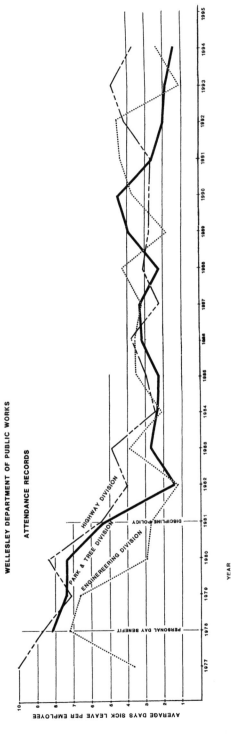

Fig. 18.3

decrease in sick leave can also be attributed to the discharge of one employee as a result of his sick leave abuse.

These rules were developed only after reviewing a substantial number of other policies, which entailed two years of review and nine revisions. You should therefore expect to spend some time developing a similar policy in your community. In Wellesley, although the personal day benefits approach improved the attendance records somewhat, the combined approach of benefits for those who come to work every day and penalties for those who abuse the system decreased absenteeism such that it is no longer a problem for that community.

References

Phillips, Leonard E., "Unionized Tree Climbers," *City Trees*, May/June 1989: 5.

————, "Incapacitated Employees," *City Trees*, December 1986: 14.

————, "Solving Sick Leave Abuse," *Public Works*, September 1984: 130.

19

Leaf Collection and Composting

Autumn leaf collection is a function the park superintendent is often called upon to perform. Leaf collection is extremely labor-intensive and because of its cost to the taxpayer very controversial in many communities. Yard wastes consisting of leaves as well as animal manure, wood or brush, and grass clippings can total 25 to 50 percent of a community's total solid waste during the peak summer and fall months. Many state and federal laws mandate that these yard wastes be composted rather than added to the landfill or incinerated. This has resulted in a surge in the development of composting facilities and in the number of contractors who deal with composting operations.

Composting Site Design

The selection of the municipal composting site is often a political decision and one that often meets with neighborhood opposition. This opposition derives from a lack of understanding about how the composting process works. One objection voiced against composting is the creation of leachate. However, plant waste does not create leachate problems; only animal manure wastes, while providing nutrients to the compost, could cause leachate problems. Another uninformed complaint deals with odor. However, a properly managed leaf composting operation will not generate any odor or rodent problems. The composting site might be a former landfill, an unused park, or vacant land. It must have a total acreage that breaks down as approximately 1 acre of compost site per square mile of parkland. It is more efficient to operate the entire operation at one site, but in heavily congested locations or in the larger cities this is not always feasible.

The site should be gently sloping, well-drained but hard. Surface drainage should go into a settling lagoon prior to joining normal runoff. The site should be level or on a constant slope and open so there is room to maneuver equipment and store the leaves. The leaves should be piled in windrows that are as long as the site and as high as the loaders can reach to maintain the piles. Consider building twin windrows when the leaves are being delivered to the site. At the first turning of the piles, the windrows can be combined into one. Because the most rapid amount of leaf size reduction occurs in the first month, after that time the twin piles can easily be managed as one large pile. To convert the leaves by weight or volume, remember that 250 pounds of leaves in a park equal 1 cubic yard. Leaves collected by vacuums weigh 350 pounds per cubic yard and 450 pounds in a trash compactor. Six cubic yards of leaves in a park will eventually become about 1 cubic yard of composted leaf mold.

Size reduction can also be accomplished by shredding the leaves prior to composting. This will reduce the amount of time needed to complete the composting process by almost 50 percent. Shredded leaves can also be used as a mulch without composting. Unfortunately, the leaves have to be replaced annually, and the decomposition process has been known to rob the soil and plants of nutrients. Large pieces of shredded leaves can also be blown away if the leaves are located at a windy site.

Management

The most effective ways to reduce park department costs in the collection of leaves is to increase mechanization and decrease labor. The leaf collection process can be the biggest and most costly municipal operation during the fall months.

The process begins by raking leaves into windrows or piles where they can be loaded for removal and transportation to the compost facility. The type of row or pile used depends upon the type of machine available for picking up the leaves. For example, vacuum machines, either self-contained, tow-behind, or attached to a truck (see Fig. 19.1) are all effective for picking up windrows or piles. Vacuums also reduce the leaf volume by 500 percent although they do not work as well when the leaves are wet. There are also new machines available that bale the leaves like a hay-baler; and auger machines that pick up leaves and move them like snowblowers. All these machines also work well for picking leaves up from windrows. Some cities use a trash packer to accept the leaves and haul them to the compost pile. The packer compresses leaves to approximately half their volume when piled in the park. Front-end loaders are slow but work well if the leaf piles are wet or frozen.

Bags are used by many communities to help homeowners and landscapers dispose of leaves in a convenient handling size. Paper bags that will deteriorate quickly have been developed specially for leaf collection, particularly if the leaves and bags are run through a shredder during the windrow processing. Plastic bags, even those with high starch content to encourage decomposition, should not be used if a quality compost is desired. If the compost will only be used for landfill cover or under sod undecomposed plastic can be tolerated. However, since most

Fig. 19.1

uses of compost are not restricted, the use of plastic bags should not be permitted until a more compostable product is developed.

An Example

A successful municipal composting operation was developed at the Wellesley, Massachusetts, Department of Public Works. This operation began with the selling of leaf dumping permits to local landscape contractors. These permits, sold for $250 per truck, allowed an unlimited use of the leaf dump from October to December. Trucks displaying the permit could dump leaves and grass clippings as often as necessary between 7 A.M. and 5 P.M. The fees collected are put into a special account, and the department can use these funds to pay for the equipment and labor for putting the leaves into windrows, turning the piles once or twice a month, and running the finished product through a screening machine. All the compost is used by various divisions within the department for routine municipal projects. No tax dollars are required, and half the leaves within the city are removed this way. The other half is removed by homeowners and dumped into windrows at a municipally run, tax-funded composting facility. However, at this second facility, the finished, screened compost is sold and delivered at a competitive price. These revenues are used to offset most of the composting costs.

Ingredients and Procedures

The making of composted leaf mold is actually a simple process, but a thorough knowledge of the process is required to ensure success. The following list describes all the ingredients required for successful composting.

1. **Air:** Loosely stack the leaves in windrows. This allows oxygen to flow through them, promoting aerobic composting and preventing a smelly, anaerobic decomposition.

2. **Turning:** Turning the row mixes the materials, aerates them, and provides a check on the progress of composting. The minimum interval of turning is four days; the more practical, however, is once a month (see Fig. 19.2).

3. **Nutrients:** Nitrogen is essential for feeding the composting bacteria. The best source of nitrogen is manure. If manure is unavailable or not allowed, the next best sources are weeds, grass clippings, aquatic weeds, and commercial nitrogen fertilizer. All but the fertilizer also supply the heat required for composting.

4. **Bacteria:** Although commercial bacterial compost starters are available, the occasional mixing of compost with previously composted garden soil should provide sufficient quantities of bacteria seed. If the same site is used year after year, the bacteria can be obtained by scraping up the top inch or two of soil when turning the pile over.

5. **Heat:** The optimum temperature is 140°F (60°C), which is no problem in summer. However, composting over winter, if desired, requires a special insulation of hay or uncomposted leaves. When the temperature has cooled to 100°F, the compost action is finished. Weeds, green vegetation, and manure speed up the heating and composting action. Only the top 3 feet in the pile or row are unlikely to decompose as readily as the interior of the pile. Therefore, when turning the pile, move exteriors to the center of the new pile and the centers out to cure at the edge. The optimum temperature will also kill most weed seeds, disease organisms, and undesirable soil pathogens.

6. **Moisture:** Rainfall is generally sufficient, but a sprinkler may be necessary to supplement natural rainfall and to ensure that the moisture content remains at a wet but not dripping level.

Fig. 19.2

Turning the pile on a rainy day allows moisture to be mixed throughout the entire pile. It also provides an opportunity to utilize equipment that is not working on other outdoor projects. If the piles are close to residential neighbors, rainy day turning takes advantage of the fact that neighbors' windows are likely to be closed because of the rain. Thus, the release of odors will not cause any complaints—making for good neighbors and therefore happy political leaders.

As the composting action proceeds, the pH value fluctuates from acidic in the beginning to neutral at completion. When the compost cycle is completed, the row can be screened and piled to cure (see Fig. 19.3). Curing allows the compost to stabilize. It also converts any ammonia in the soil to nitrates so nutrients are released to plants when they are added to the garden instead of being consumed by bacteria, which continues the decomposition process.

Value of Compost

The uses for composted leaf mold are many. It can be mixed in equal parts with sand and soil to create new topsoil. Anytime it is required in construction or for greenhouse potting soil, it can be substituted for peat. It makes an excellent topdressing for turf areas and mulch in a garden, and it is an excellent cover for construction restoration. Many communities with successful composting operations no longer purchase topsoil. Other communities sell the material to topsoil companies, greenhouses, nurseries, garden shops, or residents, or use the material to promote sales of other surplus products such as wood chips and lumber from forestry operations. Some communities have a giveaway day to get rid of their surplus leaf mold while others sell it for $10 or more per yard, screened and delivered.

Compost makes an excellent amendment to the soil. It is useful for improving soil aeration and long-term nutrient releases. Compost made of different organic materials will result in a different compost in terms of its chemical and physical

Fig. 19.3

properties. The compost product will also vary according to the compost maturity. Mature compost should be very dark in color and have a forest soil smell. If the compost has a very acidic pH or there is any hint of ammonia, hydrogen sulfide, or methane the compost has not been properly made, the composting was not completed, or the pile has not been properly cured. Whatever the reason, this compost should not be used because it will be toxic to plants and will cause marginal leaf chlorosis, defoliation, leaf scorch, or death. Nutrient values of compost are low and variable. Basically, 1 percent nitrogen, phosphorus, and potassium is normal, as is a pH of 7.0. However, many more nutrients will be released over a long time period. Fertilizer may need to be added at the time the compost is being used, but continued fertilization is not necessary. In every situation, the value of the compost is greatly enhanced if a screening machine is used to produce a uniform product.

A successful leaf composting operation requires complete attention to and planning of the site selection, the collection system, the management of the materials, the utilization of the product, and community involvement and support.

References

Bulpitt, Stan, *Municipal Leaf Composting, a Solid Waste Recycling Program,* Kingston, PA: Royer Foundry, 1973.

Harrison, Robert B., and Charles L. Henry, "Judging Compost," *Grounds Maintenance,* March 1994: C10–14.

Massachusetts, Commonwealth of, *Municipal Leaf Composting,* Boston: Commonwealth of Massachusetts, 1987.

Phillips, Leonard E., "Leaf Composting Procedures," Wellesley, MA: Wellesley Department of Public Works, July 1979.

20

Integrated Pest Management

Integrated Pest Management (IPM) is defined by the organization Responsible Industry for a Sound Environment (RISE) as a system for controlling pests in which the pests are identified, thresholds are established, control options are considered, and selected controls are implemented. IPM has also been defined as the selection, integration, and implementation of pest control based upon predicted economic, ecological, and sociological consequences. Basically, IPM is a conservative pest control process that reduces the need to apply pesticides.

IPM Design

IPM is a common sense approach to pest management that consists of nine steps:

1. Identify the plant and the pest and learn the life cycles of both.
2. Monitor the pest population and the plant's injury level to determine the type of treatment.
3. Determine the level of injury and decide whether or not the injury is acceptable, whether or not it is an economic problem, and whether or not it is purely an aesthetic problem.
4. Look at the various control methods such as whether maximum use of natural pest controls and modification techniques is feasible. Will sanitation and proper horticulture solve the problem? Consider using, first, *cultural controls* such as mulch, water, fertilizer, and crop rotation. Second, consider using *physical controls* such as spot treatments with insecticidal soaps that disrupt an insect's soft

outer body covering; summer-weight horticultural oils that smother scales and other insects; and low toxicity pesticides, such as neem products (repellents and toxins derived from the Indian neem tree), insect traps, or frightening devices. Finally, consider *biological controls,* which consist of such things as Bacillus thuringiensis (Bt) and pheromones. Of the three controls, biological controls are preferred because they do not involve the use of chemical pesticides and thus promote a safer environment, better worker safety, and higher public health value. Carefully selected plant materials bred to resist certain disease and insect problems should also be used along with proper diversification.

5. Once it is determined that treatment is necessary, it should be done when the pest is in active growth yet before maximum damage has occurred.

6. Another treatment concentrates on improving plant vigor because healthy plants discourage pest attacks. Consider accepting a certain low level of pest attacks as normal. Planting the right plant in the right place will eliminate pests attracted to the wrong plant or a stressful site. Overfertilizing however, can also cause problems where sucking insects are attracted to soft lush growth.

7. Pesticide applications should be the treatment of last resort. Applications must also follow the label exactly, be correct for the specific pest, and applied only on the problem areas and only as needed. Pesticide applications must be performed by a properly licensed person using protection for themselves and the environment as well as properly functioning equipment.

8. Once a treatment has been performed, IPM requires an evaluation. Has the treatment been successful? Was the timing of treatment correct? Was the treatment the best possible combination? Was the equipment properly cleaned up after use? Did rain occur shortly after the treatment or was the wind blowing during the treatment? What about the application frequency?

9. Records should be kept and used so annual records can be compared and the effectiveness of the treatment can be evaluated.

IPM Management

IPM works very well to reduce pesticide use, eliminate abuse, and reduce employee exposure during treatments. IPM prevents abusive chemical controls yet keeps the desirable plants alive and healthy.

IPM in turf grass management follows the same principles as IPM in other plants. For example, a seed mix is selected that is resistant to many diseases and insect attacks. One excellent mix would be Glade, Cynthia, and Rugby bluegrass with Regal perennial ryegrass. These new varieties have excellent disease and insect tolerance. A soil test to determine if problems might occur will also be necessary for turf grass management. Also evaluate the soil texture and type. Heavy clay soils, compaction, and low aeration, for example, contribute to disease and insect problems because poor oxygen diffusion from compact soil weakens the grass and allows problems to develop.

Endophytes are fungi that live in certain grass plants and protect these grasses from insect damage. Turf grass breeders are currently developing a whole new generation of turf grasses with endophytes bred into the plant. This emerging turf management tool will become much more important in the near future.

Mowing and watering of turf grass must be carefully monitored. For example, mowing at 3 inches high reduces disease attacks and prevents weed seed from germinating. The mowing should be frequent, mower blades sharp, and the clippings left on the soil. The mowing pattern should be changed frequently. Watering should be performed as needed to reduce stress on the grass and if done by irrigation, it should be performed twice a week, a ½ inch at a time. Brown grass in summer heat reflects a normal dormancy function of grass. It is not harmful and is a viable option to trying to keep grass green.

Fertilizer should be a slow-release type applied four times a year. In shady locations, the recommended rate should be cut in half. Sites with a thatch layer more than 2½-inches thick should be aerated. Weed control should be done by spot treatment. Insecticides should be specific and only applied if the pest population has increased to problem levels. Consideration should also be given to the use of biostimulants (see Chap. 13). They are a relatively new plant management tool, and more and more of them are currently on the market. Current information about them is readily available in trade journals and from product representatives.

IPM People

Despite the efforts of many organizations, environmentalists will continue their efforts to eventually ban the use of practically every pesticide in use today. Park directors should pave the way for IPM by avoiding the use of pesticides except to protect very special plants and by spraying only as needed and with the safest products available. The list of available herbicides, insecticides, and fungicides changes every year, so the pesticide applicator needs to stay current on EPA, state, and locally approved products. Sound management, inspection, monitoring, inventory control, and keeping up to date by reading trade journals and attending conferences represent much better means for controlling pests in turf areas than depending on pesticides.

References

diSalvo, Carol, "Practical IPM Programs," *City Trees,* January/February 1990: 19.

Hartman, John, "Controlling Diseases in Landscape Plants," *Landscape Management,* May 1991: 38.

Smith, Deborah, and Starton Gill, "Anatomy of an IPM Program," *Landscape Management,* August 1987: 46.

Smith, Ronald C., "IPM on Home Lawns," *Landscape Management,* December 1993: B-27.

PART 3
Plant Material

21

Recommended Annuals and Perennials

Park managers unfamiliar with plants should visit their local nurseries or garden centers several times each season. They should see what is in bloom and imagine how it will look at their site. By doing this several times a year, a flowering sequence can be established. Listed below are recommended low-maintenance annuals, perennials, ornamental grasses, and spring bulbs that thrive in harsh sites with low municipal maintenance and will do well in most of the United States and Canada. The annuals and perennials recommended here are described in detail in the Appendix. Brief descriptions of the recommended ornamental grasses can be found in the list of all available grasses presented in Chap. 22.

Recommended Low-Maintenance Annuals

Botanical name	Common name
Ageratum houstonianum	Flossflower
Begonia semperflorens	Fiberous or Wax Begonia
Begonia tuberosa hybrid	Nonstop Begonia
Brassica oleracea	Flowering Kale or Ornamental Cabbage
Canna x generalis	Common Garden Canna
Catharanthus roseus	Periwinkle, Vinca, or Myrtle
Cineraria maritima	Dusty Miller
Impatiens "New Guinea"	New Guinea Impatiens
Impatiens wallerana	Wallerana Impatiens

Kochia childsii	Burning Bush
Lobularia maritima	Alyssum
Pelargonium x hortorum	Geranium
Petunia x hybrida	Multiflora Petunia
Salvia farinacea	Victoria Salvia
Salvia splendens	Scarlet Salvia
Tagetes patula	French Marigold

Recommended Perennials

Botanical name	*Common name*
Achillea filipendulina	Moonshine Yarrow
Alchemilla mollis	Lady's Mantle
Anemone japonica	September Charm Anemone
Armeria maritima	Common Thrift
Aster x frikartii	Wonder of Staffa Aster
Astilbe arendsii	Diamond Astilbe
Astilbe simplicifolia	Sprite Astilbe
Chrysanthemum maximum	Shasta Daisy
Chrysanthemum rubellum	Clara Curtis Daisy
Chrysogonum virginianum	Mark Viette Golden Star
Coreopsis verticillata	Moonbeam Coreopsis
Corydalis lutea	Yellow Bleeding Heart
Dicentra eximia alba	White-Fringed Bleeding Heart
Dicentra luxuriant	Fringed Bleeding Heart
Digitalis ambigua (grandiflora)	Perennial Foxglove
Echinacea purpurea	White Swan Coneflower
Epimedium x rubrum	Red Barrenwort
Gaillardia x grandiflora	Goblin Dwarf Blanketflower
Galium ordatum	Sweet Woodruff
Heliopsis scabra	Summer Sun Sunflower
Hemerocallis "Hyperion"	Hyperion Daylily
Hemerocallis "Stella D'Oro"	Stella D'Oro Daylily
Hosta montana	Aureo-Marginata Plantain Lily
Hosta sieboldiana	Elegans Plantain Lily
Iris pallida	Oris Iris
Liriope spicata	Lily Turf
Malva alcea fastigiata	Hollyhock Rose Mallow
Oenothera missouriensis	Ozark Sundrop Primrose

Perovskia atriplicifolia	Russian Sage
Phlox maculata alpha	Wild Sweet William or Wedding Phlox
Phlox paniculata	Summer Phlox
Rudbeckia fulgida	Goldstrum Black-eyed Susan
Salvia nemerosa	East Friesland Meadow Sage
Scabiosa caucasica	Butterfly Blue Pincushion Flower
Sedum spectabile (purpureum)	Autumn Joy Sedum
Veronica longifolia	Sunny Border Blue Veronica
Yucca filamentosa "vareigata"	Gold Sword Yucca

Recommended Ornamental Grasses

Botanical name	*Common name*
Calamagrostis acutiflora stricta	Feather Reed Grass
Chasmanthium latifolium	Northern Sea Oats
Deschampsia caespitosa	Tufted Hair Grass
Elymus arenarius	European Dune Grass
Erianthus ravennae	Ravenna Grass
Festuca ovina glauca	Blue Fescue
Helictotrichon sempervirens	Blue Oat Grass
Imperata cylindrica "Red Baron"	Japanese Blood Grass
Miscanthus floridulus	Giant Chinese Silver Grass
Miscanthus sinensis gracillimus	Maiden Grass
Miscanthus sinensis silberfeder	Silver Feather Grass
Miscanthus sinensis zebrinus	Zebra Grass
Molinia caerulea variegata	Variegated Moor Grass
Panicum virgatum "Haense Hermes"	Switch Grass
Pennisetum alopecuroides	Fountain Grass
Phalaris arundinacea picta	Ribbon Grass

Spring Bulbs

Some excellent perennial bulbs to use for naturalizing include the following.

Allium species and cultivars prefer full sun.
Anemone blanda ("White Splendour" or "Blue Star") is a little bulb that does equally well in sun or partial shade.
Chionodoxa "Luciliae" will thrive in bare soil around the base of trees.
Crocus species and large flower varieties will flower for years in one spot.
Eranthis species likes sunny and partial shade spots.
Fritillaria meleagris (Snake's Head Fritillaria) does very well in a damp meadow.

Fig. 21.1

Galanthus nivalis is excellent for naturalizing.

Hyacinths (multiflora) are extremely fragrant and are beautiful in early spring growing in a shrub bed.

Muscari armeniacum (Grape Hyacinth) likes full sun and spreads easily by seed.

Narcissus (cyclamineus) are daffodils with small flowers and are especially recommended for naturalizing.

Narcissus with large flowers do very well in full sun.

Puschkinia libanotica does very well scattered among trees, shrubs, and bare soil.

Scilla campanulata and *Scilla tubergeniana* grow well in grass, flower early, and fade before the grass needs mowing.

Scilla nutans and *Scilla siberica* do well among trees and bare soil.

Tulipa varieties include kaufmanniana, fosteriana, and greigii.

Because there are so many new varieties of annuals, perennials, and ornamental grasses introduced every year, park superintendents are encouraged to keep up to date on the newest cultivars that are cold- and wet-hardy, pest-resistant, long-flowering, and require low maintenance. Information on these new plants comes from growers, catalogs, conferences, personal experience, and inspection of good local gardens (see Fig. 21.1). There are approximately 100 All-American Selection demonstration gardens and test gardens across North America. These gardens evaluate new varieties every year. Study the plants doing well at your nearest garden.

22

Ornamental Grasses

This chapter provides a listing of commercially available ornamental grasses as of this writing. New grasses are becoming available every year, and landscape professionals must keep up to date on the best plants for their regions. The zones given in each entry correspond to a hardiness map shown as Fig. 22.1.

Acornus gramineus variegatus
  Variegated Sweet Flag
  Zones 4–9
  6 to 12 inches tall

This plant likes sun to partial shade and needs moisture; green leaves, edged in white; will grow at water's edge.

Alopecurs pratensis aureus
  Yellow Foxtail
  Zones 6–9
  12 inches tall

Plant likes full sun; does best in mass plantings; golden foliage, arching leaves, purple-green spikes in spring.

Andropogon gerardii
  Poverty Grass
  Zone 4
  4 to 6 feet tall

Plant has big blue stems that are useful in groups for sunny locations.

Andropogon scoparius
  Beard Grass
  Zone 4
  2 to 3 feet tall

This plant has smaller blue stems.

PLANT HARDINESS ZONE MAP

Fig. 22.1

Arundinaria variegata
   Dwarf Bamboo
   Zone 4
   2 to 3 feet tall

This bamboo has broadly variegated white leaves.

Bouteloua curtipendula
   Nodding Mosquito Grass
   Zone 5
   30 inches tall

This plant has arched blades and flowers from July to November.

Bouteloua gracilis
   Mosquito Grass
   Zone 4
   1 to 2 feet tall

This grass has very narrow leaves with tall flower spikes that are good in dried arrangements.

Briza media
   Common Quaking Grass
   Zone 4
   2 to 3 feet tall

Plant tolerates poor soil; blooms are purple, spiked flowers in spring that look like oats; flat leaves; is good for dried arrangements.

Calamagrostis acutiflora stricta
  Feather Reed Grass
  Zones 5–9
  4 to 5 feet tall

Plumes in June turn brown by fall and through winter; very upright and good for screening.

Carex conica variegata
  Miniature White Edge Sedge
  Zone 5
  15 to 18 feet tall

This plant needs moisture and sun; makes mounds of arching leaves that are green- and silver-edged; excellent in a rock garden.

Carex flagellifera
  Orange Sedge
  Zone 6
  2 to 3 feet tall

Plant likes shade; rusty orange, grasslike blades that are narrow; good for a rock garden.

Carex grayi
  Morning Star Sedge
  Zone 6
  8 feet tall

This plant likes light shade to full sun; has yellow-green foliage and star-shaped heads in summer.

Carex morrowii aureo-variegata
  Variegated Sedge Grass
  Zones 5–9
  8 to 10 inches tall

Plant spreads 24 inches; forms neat clumps; used as edging or specimen; has bright yellow blades with a green midvein.

Carex morrowii variegata
  Sedge Grass
  Zones 5–9
  15 to 18 inches tall

Neat, rounded clumps; cream white margins on leaves; excellent specimen or edging, spreads 24 inches; is evergreen in the South.

Carex nigra
  Black Sedge
  Zone 4
  6 inches tall

Plant is a ground cover; likes shade, tolerates sun; dark blue-green grasslike foliage; has a black flower in September.

Carex pendula
  Drooping Sedge Grass
  Zone 5
  2 to 3 feet tall

Plant prefers moist soil and shade; tolerates sun; flowers in May to summer; coarse, arching dark green leaves; a good ground cover.

Carex stricta "Bowles Golden"
  Bowles Golden Sedge
  Zones 5–9
  2 feet tall

This plant spreads 18 inches; shade-tolerant; accent; prefers sun and moist soil; arching yellow leaves are green in spring and at the crown; fluffy flowers are creamy and silver; is buff in autumn.

Chasmanthium latifolium
  Northern Sea Oats
  Zones 5–9
  3 to 4 feet tall

Plant will grow in sun or shade; plant in masses or groups; flower has nodding spikelets in fall.

Cortaderia selloana
  Pampas Grass
  Zones 7–10
  10 to 12 feet tall

Showy accent plant with 5-to-6-foot spread; creamy white plumes; forms immense clumps; is good for dried flowers.

Cortaderia selloana pumila
  Dwarf Pampas Grass
  Zones 7–10
  5 to 6 feet tall

Plant likes full sun; tolerates most soils and light conditions; creamy plumes in late summer; use as a border or accent; withstands heat and drought; good for dried arrangements.

Cortaderia selloana "Rendatleri"
  Pink Pampas Grass
  Zones 7–10
  10 feet tall

Arching rosy plumes are one-sided and more erect than the species.

Deschampsia caespitosa
  Tufted Hair Grass
  Zone 4
  24 to 30 inches tall

Plant prefers sun to partial shade; use in masses; very graceful; needs damp soil; interesting in fall and winter.

Deschampsia caespitosa "Goldstaub"
  Gold Dust Tufted Hair Grass
  Zones 4–8
  12 inches tall

Striking and beautiful dense mounds; narrow, dark green leaves; flowers are clouds of tan; excellent in front of perennials or shrubs; spreads to 24 inches; evergreen to Zone 6.

Elymus arenarius
  European Dune Grass
  Zone 4
  2 to 3 feet tall

Plant likes sun and sandy soil; has blue foliage with wide blades; vigorous growth.

Elymus racemosus glaucus
  Blue Lyme Grass
  Zones 4–9
  24 to 36 inches tall

Plant tolerates drought; vigorous grower; likes sandy soil; has arching blades of silvery, pale blue color all season.

Erianthus contortus
  Plume Grass
  Zone 4
  4 to 5 feet tall

Stalks arch gracefully in summer and it makes an excellent specimen.

Erianthus ravennae
  Ravenna Grass
  Zone 5
  10 to 12 feet tall

Silvery-white plumes look like Pampas grass but hardier; coarse fibrous roots; good for borders and back grounds; has stout tufts.

Fargesia murielae
  Hardy Clump Bamboo
  Zones 4–9
  8 to 12 feet tall

Plant is not evasive; weeping dark green leaves; it likes most soils and light to partial shade.

Festuca alpina
  Alpine Fescue
  Zone 6
  12 inches tall

Plant likes sun; tall clumps of dark green, grasslike foliage; plant in masses; good for borders.

Festuca amethystina
  Blue Sheeps Fescue
  Zones 4–9
  8 to 12 inches tall

Very fine blue foliage with pointed tassels; this plant likes sun and should be planted in masses.

Festuca ovina glauca
  Blue Fescue
  Zones 4–9
  6 to 8 inches tall

Plant likes sunny and sandy locations; good in mass plantings and borders; neat clumps; bluest of all garden plants.

Glyceria maxima variegata
  Ribbon Grass
  Zone 4
  18 inches tall

Creamy and green variegated blades; tolerates wet and dry areas.

Hakonechloa macra-aureola
  Zones 5–9
  12 inches tall

Arching leaves are variegated with white and gold and develops a reddish tint with age; reddish flower in fall; likes dense shade but tolerates sun; likes moist soil with high organic content; is slow growing.

Heirochloe odorata
  Sweet Grass
  Zone 6
  15 to 18 inches tall

Arching green blades have subtle fragrance when crushed.

Helictotrichon sempervirens
  Blue Oat Grass
  Zones 4–8
  18 to 24 inches tall

Very showy year-round; does best in well-drained dry spots; has stiff leaves; used in borders with perennials; likes full sun; flowers in May; is not aggressive.

Holcus lanatus (mollis) variegata
   Variegated Velvet Grass
   Zone 6
   8 inches tall

This ground cover must be planted in masses; tolerates poor dry soil in sun or shade; forms a mat; has green and white grasslike foliage.

Hystrix patula
   Bottle Brush Grass
   Zone 6
   3 feet tall

Plant does best in sun, groups, and dry locations.

Imperata cylindrica "Red Baron"
   Japanese Blood Grass
   Zones 5–10
   1 to 2 feet tall

Blades change from green at base to bloodred at top; very attractive with sun behind plant; likes well-drained soil in full sun; plant in groups; will spread 12 to 15 inches.

Juncus effusus
   Common Rush
   Zone 5
   12 to 24 inches tall

Native plant with dark green spikes; prefers wet soil but tolerates dry sites.

Koeleria glauca
   Blue Hair Grass
   Zone 5
   8 to 12 inches tall

Low mounds of blue-gray foliage; likes sun and dry soil; plant in masses.

Luzula nivea
   Snowy Woodrush
   Zone 6
   2 feet tall

Dark green leaves; does well in shady areas and rocky locations.

Luzula pilosa
   Hairy Woodrush
   Zone 6
   1 foot tall

Plant is useful in semishade and is the smallest of the woodrushes.

Luzula sylvatica
   Greater Woodrush
   Zone 6
   15 inches tall

Dwarf grass with wide blades; likes shade.

Medica ciliata
   Harry Millet
   Zones 4–9
   2 feet tall

Flowers in June with cottony spikes; round habit; good for edging; graceful stems.

Miscanthus floridulus
Giant Chinese Silver Grass
Zone 5
8 to 12 feet tall

Plant used for screen or specimen; has silver spikes.

Miscanthus sinensis
Graziella
Zones 5–9
5 feet tall

Silky rose bloom fades from silver to reddish color in fall; graceful shape like vase; excellent specimen; a 4-foot spread.

Miscanthus sinensis
Japanese Silver Grass
Zones 4–9
4 to 5 feet tall

Plant's plumes are 7-to-9-feet tall; good for windbreak or background plant; likes sun; graceful branches turn gold in fall and winter; flower heads are white; leaves are tinged pink.

Miscanthus sinensis
Morning Light
Zones 5–9
4 to 5 feet tall

Narrow silver, variegated blades of light green and white margins; bronze flower head; good for winter and dried arrangements.

Miscanthus sinensis "Cabaret"
Cabaret Silver Grass
Zones 7–9
6 to 8 feet tall

Arching leaves are 1-inch wide; green with cream stripe; white feathery flowers in fall; use as specimen.

Miscanthus sinensis condensatus
"Coastal Eulalia"
Zone 6
6 feet tall

Erect stems and blades; tassels are golden in fall and winter.

Miscanthus sinensis gracillimus
Maiden Grass
Zones 4–9
7 feet tall

Plant has narrow, gray-green leaves; very graceful, creamy flowers in September; good with shrubs and dried arrangements; spreads 4 feet wide; likes full sun and any good soil.

Miscanthus sinensis purpurescens
Red-Leaved Miscanthus
Zones 5–9
4 to 5 feet tall

Foliage turns purple-red as summer progresses; reddish plumes in fall; likes full sun.

Miscanthus sinensis silberfeder
Silver Feather Grass
Zones 5–10
5 to 6 feet tall

Arching sprays of silky white plumes are 9 feet tall; good for borders, masses, or screens; clumps; is not evasive.

Miscanthus sinensis strictus
  Porcupine Grass
  Zones 5–9
  9 feet tall

Foliage has yellow bars alternating every 6 inches.

Miscanthus sinensis variegatus
  Striped Japanese Silver Grass
  Zones 5–10
  4 to 6 feet tall

White and green stripes are very attractive; soft cream flowers; use as accent or on edge of water.

Miscanthus sinensis zebrinus
  Zebra Grass
  Zones 5–9
  6 to 8 feet tall

Green blades have horizontal bands of yellow; plant at water's edge.

Molinia caerulea altissima
  Moor Grass
  Zone 6
  6 to 7 feet tall

Large seed heads turn gold from fall to winter.

Molinia caerulea variegata
  Variegated Moor Grass
  Zone 6
  6 to 8 feet tall

Cream and green variations on leaves; 15-inch flower tassels.

Ophiopogon planiscapus nigrescans
  Zones 6–10
  6 inches tall

Plant has black leaves; good ground cover; spreads slowly; use to accent bright colors; pink flowers; black fruit; heat- and drought-resistant; likes moist soil in sun or partial shade.

Panicum virgatum "Haense Hermes"
  Switch Grass
  Zone 6
  4 to 5 feet tall

Plant has wide, feathery panicles; striking bronze foliage in fall; good fall flowers.

Pennisetum alopecuroides
  Fountain Grass
  Zones 5–9
  2 to 3 feet tall

Slender arching leaves, spread 3 feet wide; large tassels are green in summer and turn brown in fall and tan in winter; graceful; use for cut flowers; likes full sun.

Pennisetum alopecuroides compressum
  Dwarf Fountain Grass
  Zone 5
  24 inches tall

Similar to the species but shorter; narrow blades; likes sun; plant in masses; has purple seed spikes.

Pennisetum alopecuroides viridescens
    Zone 5
    12 inches tall

Medium-green foliage mats in neat groups with black flower spikes.

Pennisetum orientale
    Hardy Oriental Fountain Grass
    Zones 7–9
    2 to 3 feet tall

Slender arching leaves; flowers June to October; long spikes are white; turns pink in fall.

Pennisetum rueppoli
    Fountain Grass
    Zones 4–9
    4 feet tall

Purple spikes turn coppery-red and rose; looks like a fountain.

Phalaris arundinacea picta
    Ribbon Grass
    Zones 4–9
    2 to 3 feet tall

Blades are striped white and green; good for fast cover in bad soil; invasive; tolerates wet soil and shade.

Phalaris arundinacea tricolor
    Tricolor Grass
    Zone 4
    3 feet tall

Fine textures; foliage is pink, white, and green.

Sasa pygmae
    Dwarf Bamboo
    Zone 6
    18 inches tall

Plant is a vigorous grower with green foliage.

Sesleria culumnalis
    Autumn Moor Grass
    Zones 5–8
    12 inches tall

Chartreuse clumps; use in borders and edges; good ground cover; likes full sun.

Sisyrinchium augustifolium
    Blue-Eyed Grass
    Zone 6
    6 to 10 inches tall

Blue-violet flower with white and gold center from May to July; spreading ground cover; tolerates most soil.

Sorghastrum avenaceum
    Indian Grass
    Zone 6
    4 to 6 feet tall

Plant in sunny locations in groups or masses.

Spodiopogon sibiricus
    Silver Spike Grass
    Zone 6
    4 to 5 feet tall

Dark green foliage reddens in late fall; silver spikes in summer and fall.

Stipa pennata — Feathery spikes over fine blades.
   Feather Grass
   Zone 6
   2 to 3 feet tall

Typha angustifolia — Native likes wetlands; dark green leaves are 1 inch wide; brown flower heads in fall; good for dried arrangements.
   Cattail
   Zone 4
   5 feet tall

Uniola latifolia — Plant spreads by rhizomes; slight arching flowers in August; likes rich soil and protection from wind; tolerates shade.
   Spike Grass
   Zone 5
   3 feet tall

References

Various nursery catalogs that offer ornamental grasses.

23

Turf Grass Varieties

There are many species of grasses, but only a few can be used for turf. Each variety has its own texture, color, growth characteristics, and maintenance levels. Some varieties perform throughout a wide region, while others are restricted to specific situations. For these reasons, grass seeds are blended so that the best of each variety will contribute to a total turf cover. Unfortunately, some grasses do not perform well in blends. Some, for example, tend to dominate and form tightly knit patches to the exclusion of others. Certain coarse grasses on the other hand can make an acceptable turf, but unless they dominate the mixture they will form unsightly clumps. Grasses must be properly blended, so it is usually best to select a blend developed by a reputable seed company. It is also important that any grass selection be completely compatible with the area in which it is grown. Borderline varieties should be eliminated. As with trees, be sure to select the right plant for the right spot.

Bahiagrass (Paspalum notatum) is a warm-season grass that forms a coarse, open turf that can stand the abuse of heavy traffic (see Fig. 23.1). Its deep root system allows the plant to thrive in dry, sandy soils. It is considered to be a low-maintenance grass and is often used on playgrounds, parks, roadsides, and similar areas. Bahiagrass can survive with neglect, but with care it will perform as an attractive tight-knit turf. Bahiagrasses are coarse-textured, medium-green in color, and spread by tillers and short, stocky rhizomes. Although the root system of Bahia does provide excellent drought tolerance, the turf performs best in areas with well-distributed rainfall. Bahia grows well in the shade but has little salt-tolerance. Disease and insects are also capable of causing extensive damage.

To achieve a well-groomed appearance, Bahiagrass should be mowed between 2 and 3 inches high with a sharp rotary mower. During the period when tall unsightly seed heads are being produced, a mowing interval of two times per week may be necessary. A good fertilization program is essential to maintaining a vigorous, dense turf.

There are several strains available today, including Argentine, Paraguay, Pensacola, and Wilmington. Many new strains are under development.

Bentgrass (Agrostis spp) has been the standard grass on cool-season golf courses for many years (see Fig. 23.2). Its low growth habit makes it ideal for the extremely low cut required on greens and tees. Bentgrass is extremely aggressive and generally crowds out all other grasses except Poa annua. Maintenance requirements for bentgrass are considered to be exceptionally high, and the use of special equipment is generally required. For these reasons, it is seldom recommended for turf other than golf courses.

Bentgrasses are light to dark green in color, fine in texture, and spread by extensive stoloniferous growth, which causes excessive intertwining and matting. On golf greens, a continual process of cutting and slicing is necessary to keep the turf open. This permits the penetration of moisture, oxygen, and nutrients into the soil. It also allows the escape of the harmful gases and removal of excessive thatch that becomes a problem with bentgrass. Bentgrass is susceptible to most turf grass diseases.

For best performance, bentgrass should be mowed between ¼ and 1 inch at one- to two-day intervals. A complete program of fertilization, fungicides, and insecticides is needed to keep this grass at peak performance. Water is also extremely important. Bentgrass probably requires more constant attention and care than any other turf grass. There are three varieties of bentgrass.

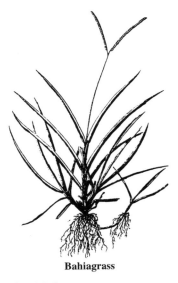

Bahiagrass

Fig. 23.1

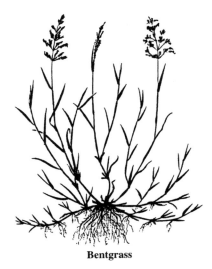

Bentgrass

Fig. 23.2

Colonial Bentgrass (A. tenuis) is fine-textured and blue-green in color. Colonial grows more upright than either creeping or velvet bentgrass. This grass is occasionally used in home lawn mixtures, but its competitiveness enables it to dominate other desirable grasses. Colonial bentgrass generally develops less thatch, but its upright growth habit makes it more vulnerable to scalping. Highland is a currently available strain.

Velvet Bentgrass (A. caninia) is fine-textured and light green in color. This grass is well adapted to cool, humid regions of the United States. Velvet bentgrass cannot withstand high daytime temperatures and is quite susceptible to drought. The most common and best-known variety is Kingston.

Creeping Bentgrass (A. palustris) is fine-textured and medium to dark green in color. It is well adapted for putting greens because of its low and aggressive growth habit. This grass is propagated either vegetatively or by seed. The major varieties are Emerald and Prominent.

Buffalograss (Buchloe dactyloides) is a grass native to central United States, from the Canadian border to Mexico. It is a low-growing grass with curling leaf blades that spreads by surface runners. It can be grown from seed or sods. Buffalograss is dioecious with the male and female flowers usually on separate plants. Buffalograss will tolerate hot, dry summers and cold winters. It is best adapted to regions where rainfall is only 12 to 24 inches per year. Mowing needs vary from once every two weeks to three times a year. It grows on heavy compact soil and needs little water once it is established. It is well suited to alkaline soils. It needs less than 2 pounds of nitrogen per 1000 square feet of fertilizer per year and is basically pest-free. The grass is dull green in appearance when growing and turns to light straw during dormancy. Some new cultivars will soon be on the market that have been developed for the transition zone in the middle of the United States. Currently available varieties are Prairie and 609. There are currently no varieties known to grow well east of the Mississippi River. Its basic aggressiveness allows it to spread rapidly into areas where damage or excessive wear has occurred.

Bermudagrasses (Cynodon dactylon) are warm-season grasses, medium to dark green in color, and spread by extensive creeping stolons and rhizomes (see Fig. 23.3). Blades are fine in texture and form a tightly knit turf. Very few turf grasses are as aggressive as Bermudagrass, and this trait is useful for renovated areas and areas recovering from damage. Most strains are vegetatively planted. In cooler areas, Bermudagrass turns brown and goes into dormancy. Milder climates will allow Bermudagrass to remain green all winter long. Bermudagrass performs exceptionally well in full sunlight but rather poorly in shade, and it does have a great deal of drought and salt tolerance.

Improved Bermudagrass should be mowed at heights of between ¼ and 1 inch. In general, Bermudagrasses perform best under high levels of fertilization. There are many strains of Bermuda including Santa Ana, Tifdwarf, and Tifgreen.

Common Bermudagrass is medium in texture and forms a more open turf than other Bermudagrasses. Because seed and planting material are readily available, common Bermudagrass for lawn installation is inexpensive. Common is used mostly for home lawns and should be cut from 1 to 2 inches. In some areas, two or three mowings per week may be necessary.

Kentucky Bluegrass (Poa pratensis) is the predominant cool-season grass in the United States (see Fig. 23.4). It probably has more diversified uses than any other turf grass. The quality, color, and performance of the grass is constantly being improved, and as a result some of the new varieties are as suitable for parks, wildlife areas, fairways, and tees as they are for the most rugged athletic areas.

Kentucky bluegrasses are dark green in color with medium-textured blades. Spreading by rhizomes and tillers, they have the ability to form an attractive, tightly knit turf. Kentucky bluegrass performs best on heavy, well-drained soils with good fertility. In the heat of summer, it has a tendency to go into an off-color dormant period. A good watering program can keep it green. In the winter, it can survive severe cold weather without damage. The rhizomes provide excellent recuperative potential after excessive wear.

Most bluegrasses perform well while being mowed from 1½ to 3 inches. During hot weather, cutting below 2 inches can harm it. Bluegrasses respond to a wide range of fertilizer rates. Bluegrasses establish rapidly in the cooler areas of the United States and southern Canada. Nearly all improved varieties are developed from seed. Fall plantings are generally considered most successful because of ideal growing conditions. However, spring plantings are quite common.

Although Kentucky bluegrass is moderately susceptible to most cool-season turf diseases, improved varieties have exceptional resistant qualities. When selecting varieties for bluegrass turf, use a blend of three or more similar-appearing grass varieties so one variety's strength offsets another's weakness.

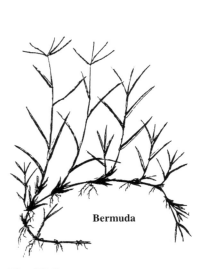

Bermuda

Bluegrass

Fig. 23.3   **Fig. 23.4**

Breeding programs have resulted in 20 to 30 varieties on the market. Some currently desirable strains include Abbey, Aspen, Blacksburg, Bronco, Chateau, Classic, Coventry, Dawn, Destiny, Estate, Huntsville, Julia, Liberty, and Princeton 104. All these strains are resistant to various turf diseases.

Centipedegrass (Eremochloa ophuiroides) is well adapted to most soils and the climatic conditions of the southeastern United States (see Fig. 23.5). It has survived as far north as northern Alabama and central North Carolina. Centipedegrass does not require a high degree of fertility and is very sensitive to nutrient imbalances, especially iron. Centipedegrasses have a pleasing dark green color and spread by thick, creeping, leafy stolons. Blades are medium in texture and form a good dense turf. It may be established either by seed or vegetative planting. Seeds are exceptionally small, so a carrier such as sand is necessary for accurate distribution.

Because of shallow roots, Centipedegrass does not have a great degree of drought tolerance. It is one of the first southern grasses to turn brown during extended periods of dry weather. This browning generally allows a thinning of the turf and an opening for weed infestations. Centipedegrass does well under moderate, shifting shade, such as is found under tall pine trees. It cannot withstand heavy traffic and recovers from damage very slowly. Centipedegrass is not tolerant of salt spray and should not be planted along beach areas. One new variety, Centennial, will tolerate alkaline soils.

Dichondra (Dichondra repens) is a low-growing perennial dicot that forms a pleasing, dense turf (see Fig. 23.6). It performs best in the warm, mild temperatures of southern California and Arizona. Dichondra produces poor growth in dense shade and does not thrive in the cool, foggy coastal areas of California. It may go off-color during cooler winter months and again in late spring when flowering and seed production takes place. Planting dichondra should be avoided in areas where heavy foot traffic or rough play are anticipated. Areas that have poor

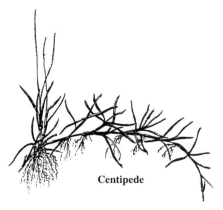

Centipede

Fig. 23.5

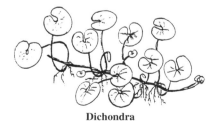

Dichondra

Fig. 23.6

drainage, lack proper watering methods and saline water are also poor risks. Dichondra has no natural resistance to diseases and insects.

Dichondra is bright green in color, with round to kidney-shaped leaves. It spreads from creeping stolons and underground rhizomes. Roots are shallow and fibrous and grow to a depth of about 12 inches. Leaves rise opposite each other, along creeping stems, and tiny flowers are formed near the soil surface. Whether you use seeds or plugs, new lawns can be started from March through October. Fertilization and frequent mowing are necessary for quick establishment. When the dichondra has filled in, mowing height can vary from ½ to 2 inches, with the most favorable range from 1 to 1½ inches. To maintain good dichondra, follow a good fertilization, and fungicide program and perform frequent proper mowing. Apply insecticides as part of a preventative program or as needed.

Fine Fescue (Festuca spp) performs exceptionally well in shade (see Fig. 23.7). For this reason, it is used extensively in seed blends designed for shady situations. It germinates rapidly, establishes quickly, and provides shelter for slower-growing varieties such as bluegrass. Fine Fescue blends well with nearly all grasses and helps give a fine texture to the turf.

Fine Fescues are medium green in color and spread by tillers or short, creeping rhizomes. They are seldom found growing in pure stands, except in areas of low fertility or partial shade. Over a period of time, Fine Fescue produces an excessive amount of thatch. In areas of full sunlight or areas requiring high maintenance Fine Fescues perform poorly. It is not considered to be as drought-tolerant as bluegrass, especially when being mowed at the lower heights. Fine Fescue is susceptible to many diseases and insects.

For best turf performance, mow regularly at 1½ to 2½ inches. Fertilization should be kept to a minimum. After Fine Fescue becomes established, it is well to start a program of thatch removal. Fine Fescues are almost always grown with improved varieties of Kentucky bluegrass. This allows the bluegrasses to dominate in sunny areas and the fescues in the deep shade.

Fine Fescues have several varieties used in turf grass:

Chewings Fescue (F. rubra commutata) is similar to Creeping Red Fescue in appearance but has a more erect, dense growth habit and no rhizomes. Chewings Fescue seems to be especially adaptable to heavier shade conditions. It will tolerate close mowing. Improved varieties include Victory and Jamestown.

Fine Fescue

Fig. 23.7

Creeping Red Fescue (F. rubra rubra) is medium to dark green in color and spreads by tillers and very long rhizomes. It performs well in open sun and moderate shade. Red Fescue is also tolerant of powdery mildew and drought. There are several improved varieties currently available including Banner, Ensylva, Highlight, Koket, and Ruby.

Hard Fescue (F. longifolia or capillata) is an improved Fine Fescue with exceptional dark green color that spreads by tillers. It also resists insect and disease damage far better than Creeping Red or Chewings. It blends especially well with bluegrass because of its excellent color. Improved varieties such as Reliant and Spartan have slow vertical growth and look good even with no irrigation, infrequent mowing, and low-fertility soils.

Sheep's Fescue (F. ovina) tolerates cold, drought, shade, poor soil, and low pH. It is desirable for poor soil settings. This grass is not good in high-maintenance areas. Its bluish, grayish color does not blend well. One variety (F. ovina glauca) is an ornamental grass that is noted for blue tufts and used in ornamental landscape beds.

Tall Fescue (Festuca arundinacea) is often used where a low-maintenance turf is desired (see Fig. 23.8). This grass forms a coarse turf that grows well in sun or shade and withstands the abuse of heavy traffic. Tall Fescue performs well in the North and is especially adaptable across the hot, dry transitional regions of the mid-South. Because Tall Fescue has a tendency to clump, it should be planted in pure stands or as a predominant part of the mixture. It has proved especially successful as a turf for athletic areas. Because the recuperative potential is slow with Tall Fescue, overseeding a few days before the heavy wear season begins will prevent bare spots and speed the recovery.

Tall Fescue

Fig. 23.8

Tall Fescues are medium to dark green in color and produce a minimum amount of tillers. They have to be seeded at the proper rate to form an acceptable, tightly knit turf. Tall Fescue is coarse, wiry, and tough. After several years, it may thin out, and overseeding will be necessary. Because of its deep root system, Tall Fescue performs especially well during periods of extreme drought. It has exceptional resistance to turf diseases and insects.

Tall Fescue performs well at a 2-to-3-inch mowing height. A sharp mower should always be used to reduce shredding of the coarse blades. Tall Fescue can perform adequately on a minimum-maintenance program. High-level feeding programs will produce an improved color and better growth response. Tall Fescue has the ability to perform well under a variety of maintenance programs and is quite often used in areas where grass is difficult to grow. It has a tendency to hold soil in place and prevent erosion, which may be attributed to very rapid germination and quick establishment.

Some currently desirable strains of Tall Fescue include Arid, Bonanza, Cimmaron, Mesa, Mojave, Monarch, Rebel II, Titan, Trailblazer, Tribute, Trident, and Wrangler.

Bonsai is a new, very durable, low-growing Tall Fescue that has exceptional pest resistance. Its deep roots require less watering and its 3-inch growth height requires less mowing. It is dark green and tolerant of sun and shade. (This may be the ideal grass.) It is available in a blend with similar tall fescues, Twilight, and Advanti.

Annual Ryegrass (Lolium multiflorum) is used in seed mixtures primarily for its ability to germinate and establish rapidly. Annual Ryegrass is considered to be an ideal component for establishing quality bluegrass turf. By germinating within a few days, it conserves moisture and provides protective shade for the slower developing bluegrass. Although a few Annual Ryegrass plants may survive for more than one season, the majority will fade away. In southern states, Annual Ryegrass is often seeded into dormant Bermuda and Bahia to provide excellent winter color.

There are three main strains of Annual Ryegrass: Common, Domestic, and Italian.

Perennial Ryegrass (Lolium perenne) is found in seed mixtures throughout the temperate areas of the United States (see Fig. 23.9). It often has a tendency to form clumps. Most improved Perennial Ryegrass has a pleasing dark green color and exceptional durability. It performs very well on athletic areas. Ryegrasses are very difficult to mow, and unless mowers are kept sharp, blades shred rather than cut the grass leaf blades.

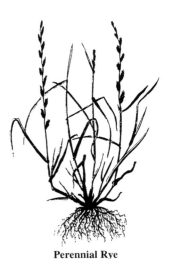

Perennial Rye

Fig. 23.9

Both types of ryegrasses are medium to coarse in texture and light to dark green in color. Improved varieties of Perennial Ryegrass are dark green and classified as fine-textured. Ryegrasses are not resistant to disease and insect damage. Ryegrasses perform well with a 1½-to-2½-inch mowing height. A moderate fertilization program is necessary for improved perennial varieties. Blends of ryegrass and Kentucky bluegrass make an excellent sport turf. The ryegrass has a high wear tolerance, and the bluegrass has an excellent recuperative potential. Perennial Ryegrasses have a large number of new cultivars, including Birdie II, Citation II, Commander, Fiesta II, Jazz, Manhattan II, Omega II, Ovation, Ranger, Regency, Rodeo, Sunrye, Taia, and Vintage.

St. Augustinegrass (Stenotaphrum secundatum) grows exceptionally well in southern Florida and from the Gulf Coast into southern Texas (see Fig. 23.10). It is extremely adaptable to these areas, retains an excellent color even after frost, and thrives with moderate care. In Texas, it blends with Bermudagrass to form an unusual turf. St. Augustinegrass has a high level of salt tolerance and thrives on soils that are almost pure sand. It is coarse in texture and spreads rapidly by aboveground runners or stolons. St. Augustinegrass performs well while being mowed from 1½ to 3 inches. New varieties are being developed that are resistant to chinch bugs and the disease called St. Augustine Decline.

Varieties of **Zoysia (Zoysia spp)** have been variously known as Manila (Z. matrella), Korean (Z. tenuifolia), and Japanese Lawn Grass (Z. japonica). These imports from tropical regions of Asia perform best in the heat of southern states but are said to be hardy as far north as New England (see Fig. 23.11). Zoysia is only recommended for and practical in southern areas. It has proved extremely successful on the golf course tees of the south central states. In the North, Zoysia turns brown with the first frost and is the last grass to turn green in the spring. It is generally planted in plugs and develops into turf very slowly. Mature Zoysia forms a mat and thatch that requires constant attention.

Zoysiagrasses are fine to medium in texture, dark green in color, and spread by creeping stolons and short rhizomes. Like other warm-season grasses, growth from dormancy occurs when daytime temperatures are consistently above 60°F. Zoysia thrives in nearly all soils and performs exceptionally well where shade and salt are problems. It is not as drought-tolerant as other southern varieties; there-

St. Augustine

Fig. 23.10

Zoysia

Fig. 23.11

GENERAL TURF GRASS SUMMARY

VARIETY	LEAF TEXTURE	SHADE TOLERANCE	DROUGHT TOLERANCE	FERTILITY NEEDS	WEAR TOLERANCE	HEAT TOLERANCE	COLOR	MOWING HEIGHT
Bahiagrass	coarse	high	high	low	high	high	medium	2"
Buffalograss	fine	poor	high	low	high	high	gray green	1"
Bluegrass	medium	low	medium	medium	medium	medium	dark	2"
Bentgrass	fine	medium	low	high	low	high	medium	¼"
Bermuda	medium	low	medium	high	high	high	dark	¼"
Centipede	coarse	high	medium	low	low	high	dark	2"
Dichondra	coarse	low	low	high	low	high	medium	1"
Fine Fescue	fine	high	high	low	medium	medium	medium	2"
Tall Fescue	medium	medium	high	low	high	high	dark	2"
Perennial Rye	medium	medium	medium	medium	high	low	dark	2"
St. Augustine	coarse	high	medium	medium	low	high	light	2"
Zoysia	fine	high	medium	medium	high	high	dark	1"

Fig. 23.12

fore, an adequate watering program is essential. Zoysia is susceptible to disease and insects. Even though Zoysia has rhizomes and stolons it does not recover well after damage or excessive wear because of its slow growth rate.

Figure 23.12 summarizes the grass varieties discussed in this chapter.

Bibliography

Scotts, O. M. & Sons Company, *Professional Turf Manual*, Marysville, OH: O. M. Scotts & Sons, 1974.

Turf Management Digest, Clarksdale, MS: Farm Press Publications, 1993.

Appendix

Detailed Descriptions of Recommended Annuals and Perennials

Recommended Annuals

(Source: California Poly. State University)
Fig. A.1

BOTANICAL NAME:	Ageratum houstonianum
COMMON NAME:	Flossflower
HEIGHT:	Up to a 30-inch mound
FLOWER DESCRIPTION:	Blue, pink, white, yellow, and salmon colors
BLOOM PERIOD:	early summer to fall
FLOWER SIZE:	¼-inch fluffy blossoms in compact, clustered heads up to 3½ inches across
SITE PREFERENCE:	Full sun to part shade in hot summer locations; any garden soil
COMMENTS:	Many cultivars; dwarf varieties excellent for borders and mass plantings, while taller varieties provide cut flowers.

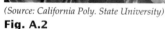

(Source: California Poly. State University)
Fig. A.2

BOTANICAL NAME:	Begonia semperflorens
COMMON NAME:	Fiberous or Wax Begonia
HEIGHT:	6-to-12-inch mounds
FLOWER DESCRIPTION:	Wide range of colors from white, salmon, and pink to red and scarlet to two colors, single or double
BLOOM PERIOD:	Continuously, summer to frost
FLOWER SIZE:	1-to-1½ inch size, single or in clusters
LEAF COLOR:	Light green to dark bronze
SITE PREFERENCE:	Moist soil, light shade; some varieties are sun-resistant
PEST PROBLEMS:	None; no damage from rain or wind

| COMMENTS: | Attractive foliage and bright blooms; use in formal and informal beds; will thrive in temperatures up to 90°F. |

BOTANICAL NAME:	Begonia tuberosa hybrid
COMMON NAME:	Nonstop Begonia
HEIGHT:	8-to-12-inch mounds
FLOWER DESCRIPTION:	Double and semidouble; yellow, red, orange, pink, and white colors
BLOOM PERIOD:	Summer to frost
FLOWER SIZE:	2½-to-3-inch blooms
COMMENTS:	Very heat- and sun-tolerant; sensational variety of tuberous begonia; grown from seed or bulbs.

(Source: Cricket Vlass)
Fig. A.3

BOTANICAL NAME:	Brassica oleracea
COMMON NAME:	Flowering Kale
HEIGHT:	Up to 12-inch mound
LEAF COLOR:	Finely serrated, notched; dark green outer leaves; red or white leaves in center expand in fall
SITE PREFERENCE:	Sunny, cool weather
COMMENTS:	Excellent accent plant; tolerates frost and heat; frilly leaves and open growth habit.

Fig. A.4

BOTANICAL NAME:	Brassica oleracea
COMMON NAME:	Ornamental Cabbage
HEIGHT:	12-inch diameter
LEAF COLOR:	Clear intense white to pink to purple center leaves; bluish-green summer leaves
SITE PREFERENCE:	Cool weather, garden soil; likes full sun
PEST PROBLEMS:	Cabbage worms and aphids
COMMENTS:	Always stays a neat mound; color lasts through hard frost; tolerates hot weather; does best if started in late summer.

Fig. A.5

Fig. A.6

BOTANICAL NAME:	Canna x generalis
COMMON NAME:	Common Garden Canna
HEIGHT:	30-to-40-inch mounds
SPREAD:	18 inches
FLOWER DESCRIPTION:	Bright colors; clusters of massive blooms on strong stems; colors range from pinks and yellows to orange and scarlet
BLOOM PERIOD:	July until frost
FLOWER SIZE:	2 to 4 inches
LEAF COLOR:	Foliage is luxuriant and bright green to bronze
SITE PREFERENCE:	Sunny, moist garden loan, add 4 inches of compost to bed each year; needs watering and weeding all summer
PEST PROBLEMS:	Leaf-eating insects an occasional problem; overwatering causes bulb rot
COMMENTS:	Propagation of tuberous rootstock is by division of tuber with one or two buds per piece. Tubers may be left in the ground in zones 7 through 10, otherwise plant after last frost and bring tubers inside before hard freeze. Husky plant with tropical foliage and large leaves. Dwarf cannas are 18 inches high, for use in borders, shrub beds, and accent spots. Cannas look best when planted in a bed of single variety plants. Mixed cannas with the tallest in the center are also an excellent focal point or border planting.

Fig. A.7

BOTANICAL NAME:	Catharanthus roseus
COMMON NAME:	Periwinkle, Vinca, or Myrtle
HEIGHT:	8-to-12-inch mound
FLOWER DESCRIPTION:	Pink or white varieties; resemble impatiens
BLOOM PERIOD:	Everblooming, May to frost
FLOWER SIZE:	1½ to 2½ inches
GROWTH RATE:	Slow growing
LEAF COLOR:	Glossy dark green
SITE PREFERENCE:	Sun or shade; moist or dry; will tolerate heat
PEST PROBLEMS:	Rarely bothered by insects or diseases

COMMENTS:	Ground cover and bedding plant, can be a perennial in frost-free areas; maintenance-free plant. Magic Carpet variety is 3 inches high; spreads to 24 inches; comes in a variety of colors that do not fade.

Fig. A.8

BOTANICAL NAME:	Cineraria maritima
COMMON NAME:	Dusty Miller
HEIGHT:	Up to 30-inch mounds
FLOWER DESCRIPTION:	Yellow flower is small and not important to plant value
LEAF COLOR:	Gray-green to silver-white; thick leaves; cut into narrow lobes
SITE PREFERENCE:	Tolerant of heat and drought
COMMENTS:	Planted for contrast in gardens. Plant is a perennial grown as a semihardy annual. Very finely cut silver-white or gray-green leaves; are similar to Chrysanthemum ptarmicaeflorum, Silver Lace or Senecio cineraria, Silver Dust.

Fig. A.9

BOTANICAL NAME:	Impatiens "New Guinea"
COMMON NAME:	New Guinea Impatiens
HEIGHT:	12-to-14-inch mound
FLOWER DESCRIPTION:	Reds, pinks, and purples
BLOOM PERIOD:	Spring to frost
FLOWER SIZE:	2 to 3 inches
LEAF COLOR:	Deep green, variegated to bronze
SITE PREFERENCE:	Partial shade, moist soil; some varieties tolerate sun and will bloom better
PEST PROBLEMS:	Spider mites and white flies in winter
COMMENTS:	Very showy, tender annual that grows year-round in frost-free areas. Tango variety was 1988 All-American Selection award winner.

BOTANICAL NAME:	Impatiens wallerana
COMMON NAME:	Wallerana Impatiens
HEIGHT:	12-to-14-inch mound
FLOWER DESCRIPTION:	Red, pink, scarlet, orange, salmon, purple, white, and variegated; prolific flower production
BLOOM PERIOD:	Spring to frost

FLOWER SIZE:	1 to 2 inches
LEAF COLOR:	Dark green
SITE PREFERENCE:	Partial shade; will tolerate sun if soil is moist; some varieties will tolerate full sun
COMMENTS:	Needs light shade in hot summer locations; tender annual; brilliant summer bloom in shady beds, borders, and containers; uniform plants. Impatiens are the most popular plant in North America.

Fig. A.10

BOTANICAL NAME:	Kochia childsii
COMMON NAME:	Burning Bush
HEIGHT:	30 inches
SPREAD:	20 inches
FLOWER DESCRIPTION:	Greenish and inconspicuous
LEAF COLOR:	Feathery, light green; maroon to red in autumn
SITE PREFERENCE:	Sunny location, warm weather
COMMENTS:	Useful for ornamental hedge; difficult to transplant unless in peat pots or small seedlings; can cause hay fever.

Fig. A.11

BOTANICAL NAME:	Lobularia maritima
COMMON NAME:	Alyssum
HEIGHT:	Up to 12-inch mound; spreading plant
FLOWER DESCRIPTION:	White, lilac, pink, or purple color; fragrant odor
BLOOM PERIOD:	Blooms from spring until frost, especially with deadheading
FLOWER SIZE:	Umbels ¾-inch around with tiny flowers
SITE PREFERENCE:	Cool weather; some cultivars are heat-tolerant
COMMENTS:	Only small seedlings transplant well; cultivars more compact than species and have larger flowers; good for edging and borders.

Fig. A.12

Fig. A.13

BOTANICAL NAME:	Pelargonium x hortorum
COMMON NAME:	Zonal or Fish or Common Geranium
HEIGHT:	1 to 3 feet
FLOWER DESCRIPTION:	Showy; ranging from white to pink, salmon, crimson, scarlet, and bicolors
BLOOM PERIOD:	Free-flowering all summer
FLOWER SIZE:	2 to 5 inches
LEAF COLOR:	Medium-green; some with zones of red
SITE PREFERENCE:	Average soil; sunny, warm spots; hot weather and humidity will cause burn out
PEST PROBLEMS:	Seed-grown plants have fewer problems and diseases; white flies in winter
COMMENTS:	Strong stems; tender perennial; grown as an annual; very popular plant.

Fig. A.14

BOTANICAL NAME:	Petunia x hybrida
COMMON NAME:	Multiflora Petunia
HEIGHT:	8-to-18-inch mound
FLOWER DESCRIPTION:	White to pink, red, purple, blue, yellow, and bicolors; fringed or wavy edges
BLOOM PERIOD:	Spring to frost
FLOWER SIZE:	2 to 4 inches; smaller than other varieties
SITE PREFERENCE:	Full sun; average, moist soil
PEST PROBLEMS:	Fewer problems than other varieties
COMMENTS:	Petunias are useful for bedding plants or specimens. They need water frequently in hot weather. Single multiflora petunias are best for long-lasting displays, and double multiflora are good for beds and containers. Double multiflora are also very fragrant.

Fig. A.15

BOTANICAL NAME:	Salvia farinacea
COMMON NAME:	Victoria Salvia
HEIGHT:	Up to 20 inches
SPREAD:	12 to 18 inches
FLOWER DESCRIPTION:	Many whorls and spikes; violet-blue with blue stalks, vivid color
BLOOM PERIOD:	June to frost
FLOWER SIZE:	½ inch
SITE PREFERENCE:	Full sun, average soil

COMMENTS:	Excellent for cutting as well as for displays and as dried flowers. Perennial is not hardy in northern United States. There are several varieties that are white flowering.

Fig. A.16

BOTANICAL NAME:	Salvia splendens
COMMON NAME:	Scarlet Salvia
HEIGHT:	Up to 36 inches
SPREAD:	12 inches
FLOWER DESCRIPTION:	Scarlet, white, and rose; brilliant spikes
BLOOM PERIOD:	All summer to frost
FLOWER SIZE:	1½ inches
SITE PREFERENCE:	Full sun in northern United States and partial shade in southern United States
COMMENTS:	Excellent for beds, borders, and edges. Each flower is long-lasting. Some varieties are free-flowering to give summer-long color with little maintenance.

(Source: California Poly. State University)
Fig. A.17

BOTANICAL NAME:	Tagetes patula
COMMON NAME:	French Marigold
HEIGHT:	Up to 18-inch mound
FLOWER DESCRIPTION:	Pure yellow to nearly red with single, double, or crested flowers
BLOOM PERIOD:	Abundant, spring to fall
FLOWER SIZE:	2 to 3 inches
SITE PREFERENCE:	Full sun, average soil; tolerates frost
PEST PROBLEMS:	Repels nematodes
COMMENTS:	Plants have many branches. Dwarf varieties are useful for beds, edges, and borders. The most easily grown annual. Vibrant colors are resistant to fading. Flowers begin as early as six weeks after seed planting. Some nonseeding hybrids flower very profusely. Many varieties have been selected as All-American Selection winners.

Recommended Perennials

BOTANICAL NAME:	Achillea filipendulina
COMMON NAME:	Moonshine Yarrow

Fig. A.18

HEIGHT:	18 to 24 inches
SPREAD:	18 to 30 inches
FLOWER DESCRIPTION:	Bright sulfur-yellow
BLOOM PERIOD:	June to September; deadhead to encourage bloom
FLOWER SIZE:	3-to-4-inch flat clusters on 18-to-24-inch stems; excellent for cutting and dried arrangements
LEAF COLOR:	Silver, gray, fernlike
SOIL PREFERENCE:	Dry, sunny, well-drained; no preference of soil type
HARDINESS ZONE:	3 through 8
COMMENTS:	Drought-resistant.

Fig. A.19

BOTANICAL NAME:	Alchemilla mollis
COMMON NAME:	Lady's Mantle
HEIGHT:	18 to 24 inches
SPREAD:	18 to 24 inches
FLOWER DESCRIPTION:	Tiny yellowish-green, on 18-inch stems in dense clusters
BLOOM PERIOD:	June to August
FLOWER SIZE:	2 to 3 inch clusters; good for cutting
LEAF COLOR:	Fuzzy, gray-green; hexagonal-lobed; distinctive colors
SOIL PREFERENCE:	Average to moist; ordinary garden soil
HARDINESS ZONE:	3 through 7
COMMENTS:	Native to northern hemisphere; prefers partial shade but does well in the sun; looks best in a mass planting.

Fig. A.20

BOTANICAL NAME:	Anemone japonica
COMMON NAME:	September Charm Anemone
HEIGHT:	18 inches
SPREAD:	12 inches
FLOWER DESCRIPTION:	Showy
BLOOM PERIOD:	Late summer to fall
FLOWER SIZE:	2 to 3 inches
LEAF COLOR:	Compound
SOIL PREFERENCE:	Rich, well-drained; partial shade
HARDINESS ZONE:	6
COMMENTS:	Prefers sites protected from wind; will tolerate full sun with ample moisture;

start plants in spring so they are established by winter.

(Source: California Poly. State University)
Fig. A.21

BOTANICAL NAME:	Armeria maritima
COMMON NAME:	Common Thrift
HEIGHT:	8 to 12 inches
SPREAD:	6 inches
FLOWER DESCRIPTION:	Lilac, white, or pink on 6-to-8-inch stems
BLOOM PERIOD:	May to July
FLOWER SIZE:	1-inch globular
LEAF COLOR:	Fine grassy clumps; dense; bright green, evergreen
SOIL PREFERENCE:	Well-drained, sunny location
HARDINESS ZONE:	4
COMMENTS:	Neat border plant; divide every three to four years or the center of the plant rots; rot is also caused by too much moisture and fertility.

(Source: Wayside Gardens Catalog)
Fig. A.22

BOTANICAL NAME:	Aster x frikartii
COMMON NAME:	Wonder of Staffa Aster
HEIGHT:	18 to 24 inches
SPREAD:	12 inches
FLOWER DESCRIPTION:	Daisylike blue with yellow centers
BLOOM PERIOD:	Mid-summer to frost but needs dead-heading
FLOWER SIZE:	3 inches
SOIL PREFERENCE:	Well-drained, moist and fertile
HARDINESS ZONE:	6
PEST PROBLEMS:	May become mildewed in humid areas
COMMENTS:	Plant 24 to 36 inches apart; full sun; needs division every two to three years.

BOTANICAL NAME:	Astilbe arendsii
COMMON NAME:	Diamond Astilbe
HEIGHT:	20 to 40 inches
SPREAD:	18 to 24 inches
FLOWER DESCRIPTION:	Feathery, pure white on 32-inch spikes; color will burn out in full sun; makes excellent cut flowers if picked when half open.
BLOOM PERIOD:	June to August

FLOWER SIZE:	Minute 8-to-12-inch clusters
LEAF COLOR:	Shiny and decorative; dark green or bronze
SOIL PREFERENCE:	Damp and lots of organic matter
HARDINESS ZONE:	4 through 8
COMMENTS:	Prefers some shade but does well in sun; use in groups of 3 or 5; tough and handsome; plants are heavy feeders and benefit from extra fertilizer; divide every three years; flower spikes last all winter.

(Source: Cricket Vlass)
Fig. A.23

BOTANICAL NAME:	Astilbe simplicifolia
COMMON NAME:	Sprite Astilbe
HEIGHT:	15 to 18 inches
SPREAD:	18 inches
FLOWER DESCRIPTION:	Light pink florets on arching plumes
BLOOM PERIOD:	Flowers freely July to early August
FLOWER SIZE:	8-to-12-inch plumes
LEAF COLOR:	Fine texture, deep green
SOIL PREFERENCE:	Wide range of soil types; moist and well-drained
HARDINESS ZONE:	3 through 8
COMMENTS:	Shade-tolerant; open airy plant; can be used in mass plantings or as an accent plant, named 1994 Plant of the Year by the Perennial Plant Association.

Fig. A.24

BOTANICAL NAME:	Chrysanthemum maximum
COMMON NAME:	Shasta Daisy
HEIGHT:	24 to 36 inches
SPREAD:	24 inches
FLOWER DESCRIPTION:	White with yellow centers
BLOOM PERIOD:	July to August
FLOWER SIZE:	2 to 4 inches
SOIL PREFERENCE:	Prefers moisture and fertilizer
HARDINESS ZONE:	4 through 5
PEST PROBLEMS:	Sometimes aphids
COMMENTS:	Prefers sun but tolerates partial shade; many named varieties; requires regular division.

Fig. A.25

(Source: Wayside Gardens Catalog)

Fig. A.26

BOTANICAL NAME:	Chrysanthemum rubellum (zawadskii)
COMMON NAME:	Clara Curtis Daisy
HEIGHT:	18 to 24 inches
SPREAD:	12 to 18 inches
FLOWER DESCRIPTION:	Pink daisies, yellow disk
BLOOM PERIOD:	July to October
FLOWER SIZE:	2½ inches
SOIL PREFERENCE:	Well-drained
HARDINESS ZONE:	5
COMMENTS:	Hardy and disease-resistant; rapidly spreading garden mum; full sun; pinch tips from stems when 4 to 6 inches tall, end of May and June; divide plant every spring and replant fleshy shoots.

Fig. A.27

BOTANICAL NAME:	Chrysoganum virginianum
COMMON NAME:	Mark Viette Golden Star
HEIGHT:	5 inches
SPREAD:	6 inches
FLOWER DESCRIPTION:	Yellow on green
BLOOM PERIOD:	All summer
FLOWER SIZE:	1½ inches
SOIL PREFERENCE:	Well-drained
HARDINESS ZONE:	5 through 6
COMMENTS:	Excellent ground cover; plant from the rich woods; propagate by seed or division; prefers sun to partial shade.

(Source: Cricket Vlass)

Fig. A.28

BOTANICAL NAME:	Coreopsis verticillata
COMMON NAME:	Moonbeam Coreopsis
HEIGHT:	18 to 24 inches
SPREAD:	14 to 18 inches
FLOWER DESCRIPTION:	Pale lemon yellow
BLOOM PERIOD:	June to frost with deadheading
FLOWER SIZE:	2 inches
LEAF COLOR:	Fernlike
PEST PROBLEMS:	Mildew-resistant
SOIL PREFERENCE:	Any well-drained; does best in full sun
HARDINESS ZONE:	3 through 9
COMMENTS:	Will tolerate drought; herbaceous; creeps by underground stems but not evasive;

very easy to grow; easily divided; selected as 1992 Perennial of the Year.

(Source: Taylor's Guide to Perennials)
Fig. A.29

BOTANICAL NAME:	Corydales lutea
COMMON NAME:	Yellow Bleeding Heart
HEIGHT:	12 inches
SPREAD:	12 inches
FLOWER DESCRIPTION:	Yellow; resembles bleeding hearts
BLOOM PERIOD:	Spring to summer
FLOWER SIZE:	¾ inch, in racemes
LEAF COLOR:	Lacy
SOIL PREFERENCE:	Well-drained
HARDINESS ZONE:	5
COMMENTS:	Prefers partial shade; grows well in gravel or rocky areas.

(Source: Cricket Vlass)
Fig. A.30

BOTANICAL NAME:	Dicentra eximia alba
COMMON NAME:	White-Fringed Bleeding Heart
HEIGHT:	10 to 12 inches
SPREAD:	12 to 18 inches
FLOWER DESCRIPTION:	White
BLOOM PERIOD:	May to June
FLOWER SIZE:	1 inch, in loose racemes
LEAF COLOR:	Fine-textured
SOIL PREFERENCE:	Partial shade, moist, well-drained
HARDINESS ZONE:	4
COMMENTS:	Divide in early spring.

Fig. A.31

BOTANICAL NAME:	Dicentra luxuriant
COMMON NAME:	Fringed Bleeding Heart
HEIGHT:	15 to 36 inches
SPREAD:	12 to 18 inches
FLOWER DESCRIPTION:	Cherry-red buds develop into heart-shaped flowers on arching sprays; deep reddish pink
BLOOM PERIOD:	Mass blooms June and October; intermittent in between
FLOWER SIZE:	1 inch
LEAF COLOR:	Medium-green and finely divided; lacy; fernlike foliage

SOIL PREFERENCE: Moist, partial shade, well-drained

HARDINESS ZONE: 3 through 9

COMMENTS: Prefers no direct sun; early spring division; U.S. Patent No. 3324.

BOTANICAL NAME: Digitalis ambigua (grandiflora)

COMMON NAME: Perennial Foxglove

HEIGHT: 30 to 48 inches

SPREAD: 12 inches

FLOWER DESCRIPTION: Spikes 30-inches tall; large yellow tubular gloves

BLOOM PERIOD: June to fall

FLOWER SIZE: 2 inches

SOIL PREFERENCE: Damp, semishade, rich, leaf mold

HARDINESS ZONE: 4 through 8

COMMENTS: Full sun or light shade; excellent cut flowers if cut when half open; divide in spring.

BOTANICAL NAME: Echinacea purpurea

COMMON NAME: White Swan Coneflower

HEIGHT: 36 to 48 inches

SPREAD: 15 to 18 inches

FLOWER DESCRIPTION: White daisylike flower with green-maroon center

BLOOM PERIOD: Mid-summer to late fall

FLOWER SIZE: 4 inches

LEAF COLOR: Coarsely toothed

SOIL PREFERENCE: Drought-resistant, sandy loam

PEST PROBLEMS: Susceptible to Japanese beetles

HARDINESS ZONE: 3 through 9

COMMENTS: Excellent cut flower.

BOTANICAL NAME: Epimedium x rubrum

COMMON NAME: Red Barrenwort

HEIGHT: 12 inches

SPREAD: 12 inches

FLOWER DESCRIPTION: Red to crimson clusters with white spurs

BLOOM PERIOD: Spring

FLOWER SIZE: 1 inch

LEAF COLOR: Dense green, evergreen

(Source: Cricket Vlass)
Fig. A.32

(Source: Wayside Gardens Catalog)
Fig. A.33

(Source: Taylor's Guide to Perennials)
Fig. A.34

SOIL PREFERENCE:	Tolerates sun; prefers partial shade; moist
HARDINESS ZONE:	5
COMMENTS:	Good for ground cover; propagate by division; cut back stems in spring.

(Source: California Poly. State University)
Fig. A.35

BOTANICAL NAME:	Gaillardia x grandiflora
COMMON NAME:	Goblin Dwarf Blanketflower
HEIGHT:	6-to-12-inch mounds
SPREAD:	12 to 18 inches
FLOWER DESCRIPTION:	Crimson with cream tips; daisy flower on hairy stems
BLOOM PERIOD:	All summer
FLOWER SIZE:	3 to 4 inches
LEAF COLOR:	Slightly hairy
SOIL PREFERENCE:	Well-drained; tolerates drought, full sun
HARDINESS ZONE:	4
COMMENTS:	Cannot overwinter in heavy wet soil; when the old crown dies new growth appears away from the center; the new growth can be dug up and transplanted.

(Source: Cricket Vlass)
Fig. A.36

BOTANICAL NAME:	Galium odoratum
COMMON NAME:	Sweet Woodruff
HEIGHT:	10 to 12 inches
SPREAD:	4 to 6 inches
FLOWER DESCRIPTION:	White tiny clusters
BLOOM PERIOD:	Spring
FLOWER SIZE:	¼-inch clusters
LEAF COLOR:	Shiny green; fragrant when dried
SOIL PREFERENCE:	Shade and moisture; well-drained
HARDINESS ZONE:	5
COMMENTS:	Excellent ground cover; does well in informal plantings, borders, or rock gardens; will die in sunny, dry sun.

BOTANICAL NAME:	Heliopsis scabra
COMMON NAME:	Summer Sun Sunflower
HEIGHT:	40 to 48 inches

(Source: Taylor's Guide to Perennials)
Fig. A.37

SPREAD:	12 to 24 inches
FLOWER DESCRIPTION:	Resembles small sunflowers; orange on 36-to-48-inch stems; excellent for cut flowers
BLOOM PERIOD:	June to September
FLOWER SIZE:	3-to-4-inch semidouble
LEAF COLOR:	Coarse texture; medium green
SOIL PREFERENCE:	Average soil with extra humus
HARDINESS ZONE:	5 through 9
COMMENTS:	Native of North America; use at back of border; sun-loving; will tolerate dry soils; durable, showy plant; propagate by seed and division.

(Source: White Flower Farm, The Garden Book)
Fig. A.38

BOTANICAL NAME:	Hemerocallis "Hyperion"
COMMON NAME:	Hyperion Daylily
HEIGHT:	3 to 4 feet
SPREAD:	6 to 10 inches
FLOWER DESCRIPTION:	Very fragrant; soft lemon yellow
BLOOM PERIOD:	Mid-July through August; prolific all summer
FLOWER SIZE:	5 inches
LEAF COLOR:	Bright green, swordlike
SOIL PREFERENCE:	Grows anywhere, sun or partial shade
HARDINESS ZONE:	3 through 9
COMMENTS:	Planted in mass; eliminates weed problems; divide every three years; received the Award of Merit from the Royal Horticulture Society; developed in 1925; one of the best daylilies.

Fig. A.39

BOTANICAL NAME:	Hemerocallis "Stella D'oro"
COMMON NAME:	Stella D'Oro Daylily
HEIGHT:	15 to 20 inches
SPREAD:	4 to 8 inches
FLOWER DESCRIPTION:	Golden-yellow on 15 to 20-inch spikes
BLOOM PERIOD:	Mid-June to late summer; longest-blooming daylily; lily-shaped blooms last only one day, but many buds on a stalk provide long bloom period
FLOWER SIZE:	2 to 6 inches
LEAF COLOR:	Bright green, swordlike
HARDINESS ZONE:	3 through 9
COMMENTS:	Use in borders or containers; multiplies

freely; extremely tough plants; plant in masses to eliminate weeding problems; divide every three years; one of the best daylilies since Hyperion and maybe best ever.

Fig. A.40

BOTANICAL NAME:	Hosta montana (fortunei)
COMMON NAME:	Aureo-marginata Plantain Lily
HEIGHT:	2 feet
SPREAD:	4 feet
FLOWER DESCRIPTION:	Pale lavender on 4-foot stems
BLOOM PERIOD:	Late summer
FLOWER SIZE:	1½ inches on stalks
LEAF COLOR:	5-inches long, dark green centers, soft cream color margin
SOIL PREFERENCE:	Moist
HARDINESS ZONE:	3 through 9
COMMENTS:	Weeds crowded out by large leaves; full sun or partial shade; plants do not need dividing.

Fig. A.41

BOTANICAL NAME:	Hosta sieboldiana
COMMON NAME:	Elegans Plantain Lily
HEIGHT:	36 inches
SPREAD:	30 inches
FLOWER DESCRIPTION:	Whitish
BLOOM PERIOD:	June to August
FLOWER SIZE:	1½ inches on 36-inch stalks
LEAF COLOR:	Blue; can get 12-by-24-inch leaf size cupped and quilted
SOIL PREFERENCE:	Moist
HARDINESS ZONE:	3 through 9
COMMENTS:	Full sun to partial shade; large, long, oval leaves; crowds out weeds; does not need division.

BOTANICAL NAME:	Iris pallida
COMMON NAME:	Orris Iris
HEIGHT:	3 inches
SPREAD:	6 inches

(Source: White Flower Farm, The Garden Book)
Fig. A.42

FLOWER DESCRIPTION:	Lilac, fragrant
BLOOM PERIOD:	Early summer
FLOWER SIZE:	2-inch falls
LEAF COLOR:	Variegated white or yellow
SOIL PREFERENCE:	Full sun; well-drained
HARDINESS ZONE:	6
COMMENTS:	Does not need mulching; propagate by division; plant the fan of leaves in the direction of future growth.

Fig. A.43

BOTANICAL NAME:	Liriope spicata
COMMON NAME:	Lily Turf
HEIGHT:	8 to 10 inches
SPREAD:	6 inches
FLOWER DESCRIPTION:	White spikes
BLOOM PERIOD:	Late summer
FLOWER SIZE:	⅛ inch on spikes
LEAF COLOR:	Evergreen, grasslike leaves
SOIL PREFERENCE:	Fertile, moist, partial or full shade
HARDINESS ZONE:	6
COMMENTS:	Ground cover; forms a thick mat; mow foliage in spring to remove brown or tattered leaves and promote rapid growth; propagate by division.

Fig. A.44

BOTANICAL NAME:	Malva alcea fastigiata
COMMON NAME:	Hollyhock Rose Mallow
HEIGHT:	2 to 4 feet
SPREAD:	Columnar 12 inches
FLOWER DESCRIPTION:	Abundant bowl-shaped soft pink on 3- to 4-foot stems
BLOOM PERIOD:	July to October; heavy bloomer
FLOWER SIZE:	2 inches
LEAF COLOR:	Deep-veined
SOIL PREFERENCE:	Ordinary soil, full sun
HARDINESS ZONE:	4 through 9

COMMENTS: Native of Europe; plant develops thick crowns with up to 50 flower stems; attractive, textured plant for middle or back of border; vigorous.

(Source: Taylor's Guide to Perennials)
Fig. A.45

BOTANICAL NAME: Oenothera missouriensis

COMMON NAME: Ozark Sundrop Primrose

HEIGHT: 6 to 12 inches

SPREAD: 4 to 6 inches

FLOWER DESCRIPTION: Red-spotted buds; lemon yellow flower; opens in evening for 24 hours

BLOOM PERIOD: All summer

FLOWER SIZE: 4 inches across; 5-to-7-inches long, funnel-shaped

LEAF COLOR: Prostrate, lance-shaped, glossy

SOIL PREFERENCE: Full sun, excellent drainage; tolerates poor soil

PEST PROBLEMS: White flies

HARDINESS ZONE: 5

COMMENTS: Wet soil may cause rot; increases by division.

Fig. A.46

BOTANICAL NAME: Perovskia atriplicifolia

COMMON NAME: Russian Sage

HEIGHT: 36 to 60 inches

SPREAD: 30 to 60 inches

FLOWER DESCRIPTION: Cloud of lavender blue on widely branching stems; 3-to-4-feet tall and wide; good for cut flowers and dried arrangements

BLOOM PERIOD: August to late summer

FLOWER SIZE: ¼-inch spikes or clusters

LEAF COLOR: Covered with soft hairs, silver-gray, aromatic

SOIL PREFERENCE: Well-drained or dry in full sun

HARDINESS ZONE: 4 through 9

COMMENTS: Plants are vigorous and hardy; use where full effect is wanted; native to central Asia; growth is branching and woody; will sprawl if planted in shade; propagate by cuttings; should be cut to ground in spring for increased vigor and better flowering.

(Source: Wayside Gardens Catalog)
Fig. A.47

BOTANICAL NAME:	Phlox maculata alpha
COMMON NAME:	Wild Sweet William or Wedding Phlox
HEIGHT:	30 to 36 inches
SPREAD:	24 to 36 inches
FLOWER DESCRIPTION:	Long-lasting soft pink-lilac on 3-to-4-foot stems
BLOOM PERIOD:	All summer
FLOWER HEAD SIZE:	6 inches, each flower 1 inch
SOIL PREFERENCE:	Moist soil and partial shade provide best sites
PEST PROBLEMS:	Mildew-resistant
HARDINESS ZONE:	4
COMMENTS:	Creeping flowerless stems increase plant size; rapid growth rate.

(Credit: California Poly. State University)
Fig. A.48

BOTANICAL NAME:	Phlox paniculata
COMMON NAME:	Summer Phlox
HEIGHT:	30 to 48 inches
SPREAD:	18 to 24 inches
FLOWER DESCRIPTION:	Rich and fragrant; wide range of colors on 36-to-40-inch stems; strong stems make excellent cut flowers
BLOOM PERIOD:	July to October with deadheading
FLOWER HEAD SIZE:	5 to 6 inches, each flower 1 inch
LEAF COLOR:	Dense and compact, deep green, lance-shaped
SOIL PREFERENCE:	Rich, well-drained
PEST PROBLEMS:	Powdery mildew and spider mites
HARDINESS ZONE:	3 through 9
COMMENTS:	Difficult to grow because of pests; grow in sun and partial shade; excellent for perennial borders; rapid growth rate.

Fig. A.49

BOTANICAL NAME:	Rudbeckia fulgida
COMMON NAME:	Goldstrum Black-Eyed Susan
HEIGHT:	24 inches
SPREAD:	12 inches
FLOWER DESCRIPTION:	Deep golden yellow
BLOOM PERIOD:	July to mid-October
FLOWER SIZE:	3 inches
SOIL PREFERENCE:	Well-drained
HARDINESS ZONE:	4 through 9
COMMENTS:	Improved cultivar of Black-eyed-Susan; compact growth; very hardy; low maintenance; strong plants; prefers full sun; does not propagate by seed.

(Source: Wayside Gardens Catalog)
Fig. A.50

BOTANICAL NAME:	Salvia nemerosa
COMMON NAME:	East Friesland Meadow Sage
HEIGHT:	16 inches
SPREAD:	18 inches
FLOWER DESCRIPTION:	Brilliant violet spikes, no pollen
BLOOM PERIOD:	All summer
FLOWER SIZE:	½ inch
SOIL PREFERENCE:	Full sun to partial shade, well-drained
PEST PROBLEMS:	White flies occasionally
HARDINESS ZONE:	5
COMMENTS:	Strong grower; excellent for low beds and borders; neat and compact plants; propagates by division or cuttings.

Fig. A.51

BOTANICAL NAME:	Scabiosa caucasica
COMMON NAME:	Butterfly Blue Pincushion Flower
HEIGHT:	24 to 36 inches
SPREAD:	12 to 15 inches
FLOWER DESCRIPTION:	Profuse, multipetal, blue, flat heads
BLOOM PERIOD:	Summer to fall
FLOWER SIZE:	2 to 3 inches
SOIL PREFERENCE:	Full sun, moist, well-drained soil
HARDINESS ZONE:	4
COMMENTS:	Propagates by seed or division; easy to grow.

Fig. A.52

BOTANICAL NAME:	Sedum spectabile (purpureum)
COMMON NAME:	Autumn Joy Sedum
HEIGHT:	6 to 8 inches
SPREAD:	15 inches
FLOWER DESCRIPTION:	Rusty red to rosy pink on 18-to-24-inch stems; long-lasting
BLOOM PERIOD:	August and September
FLOWER SIZE:	¼ to ⅜ inch, in clusters, 3-to-4-inches wide
LEAF COLOR:	Bright green, thick leaves, succulent stems
SOIL PREFERENCE:	Full sun or light shade, drought-tolerant, all soils
HARDINESS ZONE:	4 through 9
COMMENTS:	Fleshy-leaved plants; excellent cut flower; useful as a dried flower; provides winter color if flower stalk is left until spring; known in the trade as the finest upright sedum.

Fig. A.53

BOTANICAL NAME:	Veronica longifolia
COMMON NAME:	Sunny Border Blue Veronica
HEIGHT:	18 to 20 inches
SPREAD:	6 to 12 inches
FLOWER DESCRIPTION:	Dark violet to blue spikes
BLOOM PERIOD:	June to frost if deadheaded
LEAF COLOR:	Lush green
SOIL PREFERENCE:	Drought- and heat-tolerant; prefers well-drained soil in sun or partial shade
HARDINESS ZONE:	4 through 9
COMMENTS:	Long-lived plant; trouble-free; sturdy herbaceous bushes; propagates by division; named 1993 Perennial Plant of the Year.

Fig. A.54

BOTANICAL NAME:	Yucca filamentosa "vareigata"
COMMON NAME:	Gold Sword Yucca
HEIGHT:	24 inches
SPREAD:	24 inches
FLOWER DESCRIPTION:	Creamy white bells on 6-foot stalk
BLOOM PERIOD:	June to July
FLOWER SIZE:	2 inches
LEAF COLOR:	Yellow-edged, wide dark green leaves, outside edge of leaf peals
SOIL PREFERENCE:	Sandy, moist, well-drained
HARDINESS ZONE:	5
COMMENTS:	Very deep roots; practically stemless plant.

Index